Crystallization-Study
of
1 & 2 Timothy
and
Titus

Volume One

# The Holy Word for Morning Revival

Witness Lee

*Living Stream Ministry*
Anaheim, CA • www.lsm.org

First Edition, January 2005.

ISBN 0-7363-2798-3

Published by

*Living Stream Ministry*
2431 W. La Palma Ave., Anaheim, CA 92801 U.S.A.
P. O. Box 2121, Anaheim, CA 92814 U.S.A.

*Printed in the United States of America*

05 06 07 08 09 10 11 / 10 9 8 7 6 5 4 3 2 1

# Contents

# *Preface*

1. This book is intended as an aid to believers in developing a daily time of morning revival with the Lord in His word. At the same time, it provides a limited review of the Winter Training held December 20-25, 2004, in Anaheim, California, on the crystallization-study of 1 & 2 Timothy and Titus. Through intimate contact with the Lord in His word, the believers can be constituted with life and truth and thereby equipped to prophesy in the meetings of the church unto the building up of the Body of Christ.

2. The entire content of this book is taken from the *Crystallization-study Outlines: 1 Timothy, 2 Timothy, Titus,* the text and footnotes of the Recovery Version of the Bible, selections from the writings of Witness Lee and Watchman Nee, and *Hymns,* all of which are published by Living Stream Ministry.

3. The book is divided into weeks. One training message is covered per week. Each week presents first the message outline, followed by six daily portions, a hymn, and then some space for writing. The training outline has been divided into days, corresponding to the six daily portions. Each daily portion covers certain points and begins with a section entitled "Morning Nourishment." This section contains selected verses and a short reading that can provide rich spiritual nourishment through intimate fellowship with the Lord. The "Morning Nourishment" is followed by a section entitled "Today's Reading," a longer portion of ministry related to the day's main points. Each day's portion concludes with a short list of references for further reading and some space for the saints to make notes concerning their spiritual inspiration, enlightenment, and enjoyment to serve as a reminder of what they have received of the Lord that day.

4. The space provided at the end of each week is for composing a short prophecy. This prophecy can be composed by considering all of our daily notes, the "harvest" of our

inspirations during the week, and preparing a main point with some sub-points to be spoken in the church meetings for the organic building up of the Body of Christ.

5. Following the last week in this volume, we have provided a reading schedule for the New Testament Recovery Version with footnotes. This schedule is arranged so that one can read through the complete New Testament Recovery Version with footnotes in two years.

6. As a practical aid to the saints' feeding on the Word throughout the day, we have provided verse cards at the end of the volume, which correspond to each day's Scripture reading. These may be cut out and carried along as a source of spiritual enlightenment and nourishment in the saints' daily lives.

7. The *Crystallization-study Outlines* were compiled by Living Stream Ministry from the writings of Witness Lee and Watchman Nee. The outlines, footnotes, and references in the Recovery Version of the Bible are by Witness Lee. All of the other references cited in this publication are from the published ministry of Witness Lee and Watchman Nee.

# Winter Training
## (December 20-25, 2004)

# CRYSTALLIZATION-STUDY
# OF
# 1 & 2 TIMOTHY AND TITUS

### Banners:

God's economy—His household administration—
is to produce and constitute the Body of Christ
by dispensing Himself into our being
to make us the same as He is in life and nature
but not in the Godhead.

The church of God is the house of the living God,
the pillar and base of the truth,
and the great mystery of godliness—
God manifested in the flesh.

We must be inoculators, those who inoculate
others against the decline of the church,
by exercising our spirit and remaining in
the healthy teaching of God's economy.

We must be inoculators, those who inoculate
others against the decline of the church,
by being a man of God with the breath of God.

### God's Economy in Faith
### versus Differing Teachings

Scripture Reading: 1 Tim. 1:3-4, 18; 6:3, 12

*Day 1*   **I. God's economy is God's household administration, which is to dispense Himself in
Christ into His chosen and redeemed people
that He may have a house to express Himself, which house is the church, the Body of
Christ (1:4; 3:15):**

A. God's economy, as His household administration, is to produce and constitute a Body for His
Son (Eph. 1:22-23; 2:16; 3:6; 4:4, 16; 5:30).

B. The central subject of the Bible is the economy
of God, and the entire Bible is concerned with
the economy of God (1 Tim. 1:4; Eph. 1:10):

   1. The governing and controlling vision in the
   Bible is the divine economy (Prov. 29:18a).

   2. In our reading of the Bible, we need to focus
   our attention on the divine economy for the
   divine dispensing (Eph. 3:9).

   3. Unless we know God's economy, we will not
   understand the Bible (Luke 24:45).

C. Christ is the element, sphere, means, goal, and
aim of God's eternal economy; He is everything
in God's economy (Matt. 17:5; Luke 24:44).

*Day 2*   D. God's economy is to dispense Himself into our
being that our being may be constituted with
His being; this can be accomplished only by God
dispensing Himself into us as the divine life
(Eph. 3:16-17a; Rom. 8:2, 6, 10-11).

E. The economy of God is that God became flesh,
passed through human living, died, resurrected,
and became the life-giving Spirit to enter into us
as life and to dispense God into us that we may
be transformed for the producing of the church,
which is the Body of Christ, the house of God,
the kingdom of God, and the counterpart of

Christ, the ultimate aggregate of which is the New Jerusalem (John 1:14, 29; 12:24; 20:22; 14:2; 3:3, 5, 29-30; Rev. 21:2).

*Day 3*   F. God's economy is God becoming man that man may become God in life and nature but not in the Godhead to produce the organic Body of Christ, which will consummate in the New Jerusalem (Rom. 8:3; 1:3-4; 12:4-5; Rev. 21:10).

     G. According to the desire of His heart, God's eternal economy is to make man the same as He is in life and nature but not in the Godhead and to make Himself one with man and man one with Him, thus to be enlarged and expanded in His expression, that all His divine attributes may be expressed in human virtues (John 1:12-14; 1 John 3:1a, 2; 2 Pet. 1:4).

*Day 4*   H. The divine economy is to produce the new creation out of the chaotic old creation (Gal. 6:15; 2 Cor. 5:17):

        1. The history of the universe is a history of God's economy and Satan's chaos (Gen. 1:1-2, 26; Rev. 20:10—21:4).

        2. Both in the Bible and in our experience, the satanic chaos always goes along with the divine economy (Eph. 3:8-10; 4:14-16; 6:24).

        3. The Lord needs the overcomers, who will be one with Him to conquer the destructive satanic chaos and to triumph in the constructive divine economy (Rev. 2:7b, 11b, 17b, 26-28; 3:5, 12, 21).

     I. The Lord's recovery is for the carrying out of God's economy (Eph. 3:2).

*Day 5*   **II. God's economy is initiated and developed in the sphere of faith (1 Tim. 1:4):**

     A. On the negative side, to exercise faith is to stop our work, our doing; on the positive side, to exercise faith is to trust in the Lord (Heb. 11:6).

     B. Faith is a proclamation that we are unable to fulfill God's requirements but that God has

done everything for us and that we receive all
God has planned for us, all God has done for us,
and all God has given to us (John 1:16).

C. God's economy is carried out not by our doing in
ourselves but by our believing into Christ, the
embodiment of the Triune God (3:15-16).

D. Faith is a matter of seeing a view of the contents
of God's economy (Heb. 12:2):

1. Because we have seen a revelation regarding the contents of God's economy, we spontaneously believe in what we see (Eph. 3:9).

2. The ability within us to believe is a product,
a result, of having a proper view of God's
economy (Heb. 11:6, 9, 23-26; 12:2).

E. The Christian life is a life of faith, a life of believing (Gal. 3:2, 14):

1. We do not live according to what we see; we
live according to what we believe (John
20:25-29).

2. Our walk is by faith, not by sight (2 Cor.
5:7).

*Day 6* III. **God's economy in faith is versus differing
teachings (1 Tim. 1:3-4):**

A. Differing teachings refer to teachings that are
not in line with the economy of God (6:3).

B. The differing teachings in 1:3-4, 6-7; 6:3-5, 20-21
and the heresies in 4:1-3 are the seed, the
source, of the church's decline, degradation, and
deterioration.

C. Teaching differently tears down God's building
and annuls God's economy; even a small
amount of teaching in a different way destroys
the recovery.

D. For the administration and shepherding of a
local church, the first thing needed is to ter-
minate the differing teachings of the dissenting
ones, which distract the saints from the central
line of God's economy (Titus 1:9).

E. Paul charged Timothy, his faithful co-worker, to

fight against the differing teachings and to fight
for God's economy (1 Tim. 6:12; 2 Tim. 2:3-4).

F. To war the good warfare is to war against the
differing teachings and to carry out God's economy according to the apostle's ministry concerning the gospel of grace and eternal life for the
glory of the blessed God (1 Tim. 1:18; 6:12).

G. We must avoid differing teachings and concen-
trate on God's economy concerning Christ and
the church (1:3-4; Eph. 3:9; 5:32).

H. The crucial point of the healthy teaching of the
apostolic ministry concerns the Triune God processed to dispense Himself as the all-inclusive
life-giving Spirit into His chosen ones so that
they may be brought into an organic union to
receive the divine transfusion and thereby
become sons of God and members of Christ; as
a result, they can become the Body of Christ to
express Christ, the One in whom the fullness of
God dwells (1 Cor. 15:45b; 6:17; 12:12-13, 27).

## Morning Nourishment

1 Tim. Even as I exhorted you...to remain in Ephesus in or-
1:3-4 der that you might charge certain ones not to teach
different things,...which produce questionings
rather than God's economy, which is in faith.

Eph. And to enlighten all *that they may see* what the econ-
3:9-11 omy of the mystery is, which throughout the ages
has been hidden in God, who created all things, in
order that now to the rulers and the authorities in
the heavenlies the multifarious wisdom of God
might be made known through the church, according to the eternal purpose which He made in Christ
Jesus our Lord.

*God's economy* in 1 Timothy 1:4 is God's household economy
(Eph. 1:10; 3:9). This is God's household administration to dispense Himself in Christ into His chosen people, that He may have
a house, a household, to express Himself, which household is the
church, the Body of Christ (1 Tim. 3:15). The apostle's ministry
was centered upon this economy of God (Col. 1:25; 1 Cor. 9:17),
whereas the differing teachings of the dissenting ones were used
by God's enemy to distract His people from this. This divine economy must be made fully clear to the saints in the administration
and shepherding of a local church.

My burden is altogether centered on God's economy. This has
been my burden for more than forty years. During the years I
have been in this country, I have not taught anything other than
God's economy. (*Life-study of 1 Timothy*, p. 11)

## Today's Reading

The Christ revealed in the Bible is the embodiment of the
Triune God and all the processes through which He has passed,
including incarnation, human living, crucifixion, resurrection,
ascension, and descension. In such a Christ God made His eternal economy. Christ, therefore, is...the center, circumference,
element, sphere, means, goal, and aim of this economy.

God's New Testament economy is His plan to dispense Himself

into His chosen people in His trinity....This dispensing has three steps. First, it is of God the Father. The Father is the source, the origin. Second, this dispensing is through God the Son, who is the course. Third, God's dispensing is in God the Spirit, who is the instrument and sphere. Through these steps of God the Father, through God the Son, and in God the Spirit, God dispenses Himself into His chosen people.

God's New Testament economy to dispense Himself into His chosen people is for the producing of the church (Eph. 3:10). This dispensing brings forth the church for the manifestation of the multifarious wisdom of God according to His eternal purpose made in Christ (Eph. 3:9-11)....Through the dispensing of God in His trinity the church is produced to exhibit God's manifold wisdom.

Throughout the years we have given many messages on God's New Testament economy. However, according to my observation, most of the saints who have received these messages still need a clear vision of God's economy. We need a vision of the central matter in the Bible—the desire of God's heart to dispense Himself into His chosen people in His trinity for the producing of the church, which is the kingdom of God that will consummate in the New Jerusalem as the eternal expression of the Triune God.

We need a vision of God's New Testament economy. It is not adequate merely to know about it....Seeing the vision of God's New Testament economy is different from simply hearing about it. I hope that all the saints will spend much time to pray, both individually and corporately, regarding this. We need to say, "Lord, I cry out to You concerning God's economy. I need a vision of the New Testament economy...." (*The Conclusion of the New Testament*, pp. 17-19)

*Further Reading: Life-study of 1 Timothy*, msg. 1; *The Conclusion of the New Testament*, msg. 2; *Crystallization-study of Song of Songs*, msgs. 1-2, 4, 7, 12; *The Divine Economy*, ch. 1; *The Divine Dispensing for the Divine Economy*, ch. 1; *The Economy and Dispensing of God*, ch. 1; *A General Outline of God's Economy and the Proper Living of a God-man*, ch. 1

*Enlightenment and inspiration:* _____

_____

_____

_____

## *Morning Nourishment*

John
1:14   And the Word became flesh and tabernacled among us (and we beheld His glory, glory as of the only Begotten from the Father), full of grace and reality.

12:24   ...Unless the grain of wheat falls into the ground and dies, it abides alone; but if it dies, it bears much fruit.

3:3   ...Unless one is born anew, he cannot see the kingdom of God.

29   He who has the bride is the bridegroom...

The center of the Bible...is the highest vision in the Bible; it is the vision that governs and controls us. Paul said, "I was not disobedient to the heavenly vision" (Acts 26:19). What was the heavenly vision to which Paul referred? It has been at least seventy-three years now since Brother Nee was raised up by the Lord to speak for Him among us. During this period of time, not only our hearts but even our hands have never left the Bible. According to the number of pages we have touched, it is as if we have thoroughly handled a hundred Bibles. Moreover, we have many notes of what we have gained from our study of the Word. After seventy-three years, we may say that the Lord's revelation among us has reached its peak,...[which]...can be seen in the new hymn that I wrote: "What miracle! What mystery! / That God and man should blended be! / God became man to make man God, / Untraceable economy!" The heavenly vision which the Lord showed Paul was this economy, the New Testament economy, the eternal economy of God. This economy is the revelation of the entire New Testament. (*The Governing and Controlling Vision in the Bible,* pp. 7-8)

## *Today's Reading*

This is the economy of God, the New Testament revelation, the teaching of the apostles. This is the result of our study of the Word for over seventy years. This is the extract, the crystallization. The twenty-seven books of the New Testament mention many matters, but in summary they concern the economy of God. God's economy is that God became flesh, passed through human living, died, and resurrected; then He became the Spirit and entered into men to dispense God into them for their regeneration, issuing in the church. The church as the Body of Christ is His continuation, enlargement, and multiplication; it is also the kingdom of God, the house of God, and at the same time the counterpart of Christ as His bride. The ultimate consummation of the totality of all these items is the New Jerusalem.

Some may ask, "Brother Lee, I have been an elder for fifteen years, but I still don't know how to be an elder. What shall I do?" Let me tell you this: You do not know how to be an elder because you have not seen the economy of God....You have to see that God became flesh, passed through human living, died daily, eventually died on the cross, and then resurrected and became the Spirit. This Spirit enters into us to dispense God into us. If you see these things, you will know how to be an elder. If you pray over these words and let them get into you, you will spontaneously realize how to be an elder. Hence, this is a governing vision and a controlling vision. As the leading apostle, Paul was governed and controlled by this vision in all his work and actions. We should be governed and controlled also.

All the things referred to in the Bible are for the fulfillment and accomplishment of the economy of God. The economy of God is that God became flesh, passed through human living, died, resurrected, and became the Spirit to enter into us as life and dispense God into us that we may be transformed for the producing of the church, which is the Body of Christ, the house of God, the kingdom of God, and the counterpart of Christ, the ultimate aggregate of which is the New Jerusalem. This is the Bible, and this is the vision that governs and controls us. (*The Governing and Controlling Vision in the Bible,* pp. 16-17)

*Further Reading: The Governing and Controlling Vision in the Bible,* msgs. 1-2; *Life-study of 1 & 2 Chronicles,* msgs. 1, 5-6, 11; *The God-men,* ch. 1; *Messages to the Trainees in Fall 1990,* ch. 19; *Basic Training,* msg. 5; *Life Messages,* vol. 2, ch. 65

*Enlightenment and inspiration:* _____

_____

_____

_____

## *Morning Nourishment*

2 Pet. Through which He has granted to us precious and
1:4   exceedingly great promises that through these you
      might become partakers of the divine nature...
1 John Behold what manner of love the Father has given to
3:1-2 us, that we should be called children of God; and we
      are....And it has not yet been manifested what we
      will be. We know that if He is manifested, we will be
      like Him because we will see Him even as He is.
Rev. And he...showed me the holy city, Jerusalem, com-
21:10 ing down out of heaven from God.

God is self-existing and ever-existing (Exo. 3:14), and God is
triune—the Father, the Son, and the Spirit (Matt. 28:19; 2 Cor.
13:14). The Triune God has one heart's desire (Eph. 1:5, 9). According to His heart's desire, God made His eternal economy
(1 Tim. 1:4b; Eph. 1:10; 3:9) to make man the same as He is in life
and nature but not in His Godhead and to make Himself one with
man and man one with Him, thus to be enlarged and expanded in
His expression, that all His divine attributes may be expressed in
human virtues. (*The Ten Great Critical "Ones" for the Building
Up of the Body of Christ*, p. 14)

## *Today's Reading*

God carries out His eternal economy through a number of
steps. First, He created man in His image and after His likeness
(Gen. 1:26-27). Then God became a man in His image and after
His likeness. He became a man in His incarnation to partake of
the human nature (Heb. 2:14a). He lived a human life to express
His attributes through man's virtues. He died an all-inclusive
death and resurrected to produce the firstborn Son of God and become the life-giving Spirit (Rom. 8:29; Acts 13:33; 1 Cor. 15:45).
This was all for Him to dispense Himself into His chosen people to
regenerate them with Himself as their life for producing many
sons—many God-men (1 Pet. 1:3)—for the forming of the
churches with His many sons and for the building up of the Body
of Christ with His brothers as the members to be the organism of

the processed and consummated Triune God, consummating in the New Jerusalem as His eternal enlargement and expression.

We may say that we have already heard the truth concerning God's economy, but to hear is not sufficient. We have to present this truth to others, to give messages to them. Paul exhorted Timothy to stay in Ephesus to charge some there not to speak things other than God's economy (1 Tim. 1:3-4). We have to be controlled by the vision of God's economy. We should not speak anything other than God's economy. (*The Ten Great Critical "Ones" for the Building Up of the Body of Christ,* pp. 14-15)

God's economy is to make all the redeemed ones, all the believers in Christ, God-men. God's desire is not to have good men—God's desire is to have God-men. Christ, the unique God-man, is the model, the prototype, used by God to have a "mass production" of millions of God-men. Regeneration brings God into us, making us God-men. As God-men we should have a God-man's living, continually rejecting our natural man and living by the very God who is life in us. As God-men we should deny our natural life and apply the divine life in our daily life.

In his fourteen Epistles Paul did a wonderful job of unveiling how Christ as the ascended One in the heavens ministers Himself as the life-giving Spirit, as the pneumatic Christ, as the embodiment of the processed Triune God in His resurrection, to transform us from clay into something precious, making us the same as He, not in the Godhead but in His essence, in His element, in His nature, in His life, and in His appearance. This is the economy of God, which will consummate in the New Jerusalem. (*Life-study of 1 & 2 Kings,* pp. 136-137)

*Further Reading: The Ten Great Critical "Ones" for the Building Up of the Body of Christ,* msg. 1; *Life-study of 1 & 2 Kings,* msgs. 1, 4, 7-8, 17-21; *Living a Life according to the High Peak of God's Revelation,* chs. 1-2, 4; *The Divine and Mystical Realm,* chs. 1-2, 4, 6; *The High Peak of the Vision and the Reality of the Body of Christ,* chs. 2-4

*Enlightenment and inspiration:* _____
_____
_____
_____

## *Morning Nourishment*

Eph.  That we may be no longer little children tossed by
4:14-15  waves and carried about by every wind of teaching in
the sleight of men, in craftiness with a view to a system
of error, but holding to truth in love, we may grow up
into Him in all things, who is the Head, Christ.

Gal.  For neither is circumcision anything nor uncircum-
6:15  cision, but a new creation *is what matters.*

2 Cor.  So then if anyone is in Christ, *he is* a new creation. The
5:17  old things have passed away; behold, they have become new.

The first creation did not accomplish God's purpose directly.
Rather, it was God's intention to gain the new creation through
the first creation. This means that through the old creation God
will have a new creation [2 Cor. 5:17; Gal. 6:15]....We were the old
man, but we have been regenerated to become the new man, and
the new man is the new creation.

Although God created the heavens and the earth, He was not
in the old creation. This means that the old creation does not have
God as its life, nature, and person. But in the new creation we
have God within us as our life, our nature, our person, and our everything. Do we need love? Our God within us is love. Do we need
light? Our God within us is light. Do we need the divine attributes? Our God within us is the divine attributes, which will be
expressed in our human virtues. Therefore, in the new creation
God is everything. (*The Satanic Chaos in the Old Creation and
the Divine Economy for the New Creation,* p. 15)

## *Today's Reading*

God's intention is to produce the new creation out of the old
creation. The universe exists for this purpose, this goal. God created the first creation, which has become the old creation. Now
out of the old creation He is producing the new creation. This new
creation is something that is mingled with Him.

In order to produce the new creation out of the old creation,
God first came into the old creation as a man. Then He lived in the

old creation as a man for thirty-three and a half years. He died in the old creation and then was resurrected. In resurrection He became the life-giving Spirit (1 Cor. 15:45) to enter into all His believers, who were the old creation, to make them something new. This means that all His believers have received Him as the divine economy for the new creation.

Our becoming a new creation in Christ began with our regeneration, and it continues with our being sanctified, renewed, and transformed. Eventually, we will be conformed to the image of Christ and glorified. That will be the consummation of the new creation.

According to the Bible, the old creation must pass through four ages: the age before the law, the age of the law, the age of grace, and the age of the kingdom. As believers in Christ, we are now in the third age, the age of grace, expecting to enter into the age of the kingdom. God uses these four ages to gain the new creation out of the old creation.

Today the earth is filled with chaos. Chaos is everywhere. Every part of society is chaotic. However, we should not be discouraged. In addition to the satanic chaos, there is the divine economy. Whereas the satanic chaos will come to an end, the divine economy will reach a consummation. The end of the satanic chaos will be the lake of fire, and the consummation of the divine economy will be the New Jerusalem.

We need to realize that, both in the Bible and in our experience, the satanic chaos always goes along with the divine economy. It seems that we alternate between economy and chaos, between chaos and economy. Where there is the divine economy, there is the satanic chaos. Where God is, Satan is also. Satan is not behind God, following Him; rather, Satan is at God's side. We may say that God is in the "central lane" and Satan is in the "side lane." (*The Satanic Chaos in the Old Creation and the Divine Economy for the New Creation*, pp. 15-16)

*Further Reading: The Satanic Chaos in the Old Creation and the Divine Economy for the New Creation, msgs. 1-5*

*Enlightenment and inspiration:* _____
_____
_____
_____

## Morning Nourishment

1 Tim.  Even as I exhorted you...that you might charge cer-
1:3-4   tain ones not to teach different things...rather than
        God's economy, which is in faith.
Rom.    So faith *comes* out of hearing, and hearing through
10:17   the word of Christ.
Eph.    And to enlighten all *that they may see* what the
3:9     economy of the mystery is...
Heb.    Looking away unto Jesus, the Author and Perfecter
12:2    of our faith, who for the joy set before Him endured
        the cross, despising the shame, and has sat down on
        the right hand of the throne of God.

God's economy is in faith. It is not by our doing but by our faith in God's grace. It is not by our doing in ourselves but by our believing in Christ, the embodiment of the Triune God. In the Lord's ministry, we are not teaching the saints to observe something, to keep something, or to do something. We are ministering to the saints something that needs the exercise of their faith. Faith does not originate from us. Faith originates from what we see. When we see God's economy, this generates and initiates a believing within us. God's economy is God's will to dispense Himself into you and me to produce an organism, the Body of Christ, for His good pleasure. Faith comes from seeing this vision. We need a vision, a seeing. We need to see that in the whole universe God's good pleasure is to impart Himself, to dispense Himself, into us so that we may become parts of His organism, the organic Body of Christ. (*Living in and with the Divine Trinity*, pp. 19-20)

## Today's Reading

Christians often speak of the faith in an objective sense. Someone may ask what your faith is, meaning what you believe. This aspect of faith, the objective aspect, is not a matter of our action of believing, but a matter of what we believe. This objective faith includes the contents of God's New Testament economy.

When we receive a word concerning the objective faith, the contents of God's New Testament economy, spontaneously subjective faith is produced in us. We respond to the objective faith by believing....We hear of the objective faith, and then subjective faith rises up in us. This subjective faith is our act of believing.

Subjective faith does not happen once for all. On the contrary, from the time we began to believe, the action of believing has been going within us, for the Christian life is a life of faith, a life of believing. Day by day we are living a believing life. We do not live according to what we see; we live according to what we believe. As Paul says, "We walk by faith, not by appearance" (2 Cor. 5:7).

Those who backslide, including many who leave the church life, experience some loss of faith. They may not lose their faith absolutely, but they may lose it at least in part....Whenever someone loses sight of the contents of God's economy, the subjective faith, the believing action within him, also diminishes. The ability within us to believe is always a product, a result, an issue, of having a proper view of God's economy. Therefore, it is a dreadful matter to lose sight of God's economy.

In the meetings of the church and of the ministry, it is as if we are all watching a heavenly television to see more of God's economy. The more we see this heavenly television, the more we believe....Therefore,...the meetings of the church and the ministry enlarge our capacity to believe.

We all need to have a broad view of God's economy. Once we see such a view, we shall spontaneously believe in what we see.... Paul's writings take us on a tour to show us heavenly, spiritual things concerning Christ, His achievements and attainments, and what He has obtained. The more we see concerning this, the more we shall be impressed, and the more faith we shall have. We shall find that it is simply impossible not to believe. (*Life-study of 1 Thessalonians,* pp. 119-120, 122-123, 129)

*Further Reading: Living in and with the Divine Trinity,* ch. 2; *Life-study of 1 Thessalonians,* msgs. 14-15; *Crystallization-study of the Epistle to the Romans,* msgs. 7-11; *A General Outline of God's Economy and the Proper Living of a God-man,* ch. 4

*Enlightenment and inspiration:* _____

_____

_____

## Morning Nourishment

1 Tim. Even as I exhorted you, when I was going into Mace-
1:3 donia, to remain in Ephesus in order that you might
charge certain ones not to teach different things.
6:3 If anyone teaches different things and does not consent to healthy words, those of our Lord Jesus Christ,
and the teaching which is according to godliness.
Titus Holding to the faithful word, which is according to
1:9 the teaching *of the apostles,* that he may be able both
to exhort by the healthy teaching and to convict
those who oppose.

This Epistle [of 1 Timothy] is altogether an inoculation. Poison after poison was injected into the Christian church while the
church was going on. At the conclusion of his writing ministry,
Paul wrote 1 Timothy to inoculate the church against all these
poisons....[In 1:3, the] phrase "not to teach different things"
seems so simple. If you merely read this phrase, you will not
sense the seriousness of different teaching. We may not think
that this is serious, but actually it is more than serious. It kills
people to teach differently. To teach differently tears down God's
building and annuls God's entire economy. We all must realize
that even a small amount of teaching in a different way destroys
the recovery....You do not need to give an entire message. Just
by speaking one sentence, which conveys your kind of concept,
tears down everything. We must realize that that kind of ministry is "terrible." Your speaking can build up or destroy. It is possi-
ble that your speaking destroys, kills, and annuls. (*Elders'
Training, Book 3: The Way to Carry Out the Vision,* pp. 42-43)

## Today's Reading

As we have seen, Paul tells Timothy in 1 Timothy 1:3 that he
left him there in Ephesus to charge certain ones not to teach different things. What then, we may ask, is the unique thing which
all the Christian teachers should teach? Christian teachers today
teach many things....We would all agree that to teach the way of
Judaism is surely wrong, but what about teaching how to preach

the gospel? What is wrong with preaching the gospel? We must realize that even the teaching to preach the gospel creates division. This is wrong. There is only one ministry which always builds up, edifies, and perfects with no destruction at all. There is only one unique ministry that is justified, promoted, uplifted, and even glorified in the New Testament. In 1 Timothy 1:4 Paul went on to tell Timothy what those ones who were teaching different things should be occupied with—God's economy....I do not like to see the recovery destroyed by different teachings....My contact with some of you impressed me with a terrible factor. I realized that you were going to teach things differently to cause trouble and to create division. There is only one ministry that ever builds up and that never destroys—this is God's economy.

In 1 Timothy Paul did not indicate that those who taught differently taught heresies or heathen things. If they had taught heathen things, no Christian would have taken them. The reason why their teachings were received is because they were scriptural things....Their teaching, however, created division. Is there anything wrong with setting up a mission and sending missionaries to the field? We must realize that this is not a matter of being wrong or right, but it is a matter of "cutting Christ's Body into pieces." On the one hand, the bringing of people to Christ through the missionaries is very positive. Unconsciously, however, this kind of work cuts Christ's Body into pieces. We should be careful because we may do the same thing. We may insist, stress, and emphasize a scriptural item which seemingly is right, yet actually it cuts the Body of Christ. It divides the recovery. We must be careful....I am afraid that some different teachings might be on the verge of coming out. (*Elders' Training, Book 3: The Way to Carry Out the Vision,* pp. 43-45)

*Further Reading: Elders' Training, Book 3: The Way to Carry Out the Vision,* ch. 4; *Elders' Training, Book 7: One Accord for the Lord's Move,* ch. 3; *Life-study of 1 Timothy,* msgs. 1-2, 12; *Life-study of Titus,* msgs. 1-2, 5-6

*Enlightenment and inspiration:* _____

_____

_____

### *Hymns,* #971

1  God's eternal purpose
     Is to join with man,
   Causing man, His vessel,
     To be born again,
   His own life imparting,
     Filling to the brim;
   Man may thus express Him,
     And be one with Him.

2  God in His own image
     Hath created man,
   That he may be able
     To fulfill His plan;
   That he may receive Him
     As the tree of life
   To become His fulness
     As to man the wife.

3  In His life's rich flowing
     Man will be transformed
   Into precious substance
     And to Him conformed.
   Thus will man be builded
     As His counterpart,
   Thus to be His dwelling,
     Satisfy His heart.

4  'Tis the holy city,
     New Jerusalem;
   With His saints God mingles,
     Makes His home with them.
   He becomes their content,
     His expression they;
   They shall share His glory,
     One with Him for aye.

5  He's the very center,
     Ruling on the throne;
   By His life the power,
     Saints are kept in one.
   By His light of glory,
     They are kept in light,
   Harmony enjoying
     In divine delight.

6   He's their living water,
    And their food supply;
    All their thirst and hunger
    He doth satisfy.
    He's for them the temple,
    In Himself they live,
    In His constant presence
    Worship ever give.

*Composition for prophecy with main point and sub-points:* _____

_____

_____

_____

_____

_____

_____

_____

_____

_____

_____

_____

_____

_____

_____

_____

_____

_____

_____

_____

_____

_____

_____

_____

_____

_____

_____

_____

_____

_____

_____

_____

### The Function of the Church (1)
### The House of the Living God

Scripture Reading: 1 Tim. 3:15; John 14:2; Eph. 2:19, 21-22;
1 Pet. 2:5; 2 Tim. 2:20

*Day 1*    I. As saved ones and members of the church, we
need to know the church (Matt. 16:18; 18:17;
Eph. 1:22-23; 2:15, 19-22; 3:4, 10-11; 4:16; 5:32;
6:11).

II. The desire of the Lord's heart is to gain the
church; thus, we should treasure the church
and love the church, even as the Lord does
and as Paul did (Matt. 16:18; 13:44-46; Eph.
1:5, 9; 5:25-27; 2 Cor. 12:14-15):

A. God obtained the church "through His own
blood," and the church is under the care of the
Holy Spirit; this indicates the precious love of
God for the church and the preciousness of the
church in the eyes of God (Acts 20:28).

B. Because Paul's heart was fully for the church and
on the church, he was willing to spend and be
utterly spent for the church and to minister life
to the church by dying (2 Cor. 12:14-15; 11:28;
4:10-12).

III. The church is the church of God (1 Cor. 1:2;
10:32; 11:16):

A. The expression *the church of God* indicates that
the church is possessed by God and that the
church has the nature of God and is constituted
with the element of God (Acts 20:28; Gal. 1:13).

B. The church is *of* God because it is produced of
God as its source and has God as its nature and
essence, which are divine, universal, and eternal
(1 Cor. 10:32):

1. God is the nature and essence of the church;
therefore, the church is divine (Rev. 1:12, 20).

2. The content of the church essentially is God
Himself (1 Cor. 3:16-17).

Day 2  IV. **The church of God is the house of the living God (1 Tim. 3:15):**
   A. To Christ, the church is the Body; to God, the church is the house (Eph. 1:22-23; John 14:2).
   B. The house of God is the household of God (Eph. 2:19):
      1. The dwelling place—the house—and the family—the household—are one entity—a group of called, regenerated ones indwelt by God Himself (1 Pet. 1:3; 2:5; 1 Cor. 3:16).

Day 3      2. The household of God is composed of the many sons of God as the many brothers of Christ, the firstborn Son of God (Rom. 8:29; Heb. 2:10-12):
         a. The church is composed of those who have been born of God and have the life and nature of God (John 3:15; 2 Pet. 1:4).
         b. God dispensed Himself in Christ into us, begetting us as His children; in this way we have become His household (1 Pet. 1:3; John 1:12-13).
         c. The Father is God, and the many sons are God in life and nature but not in the God-head (Heb. 2:10).
      3. Just as Christ is not separate from the members of His Body but dwells in them, the Father is not a separate member of His household but is in all His children (Rom. 8:10; 12:4-5; 2 Cor. 6:16).
      4. The house of God is organic in the divine life, organic in the divine nature, and organic in the Triune God; because the church is organic, the church grows (Eph. 2:21).
   C. In speaking of the church as the house of God, Paul refers to God as the living God (1 Tim. 3:15):
      1. The living God, who lives in the church, must be subjective to the church and not merely objective (1 Cor. 3:16).

2. Because God is living, the church as the house of God is also living in Him, by Him, and with Him; a living God and a living church live, move, and work together.

3. The house of the living God is living in the Father's name and in the Father's life, that is, living in the Father's reality (John 14:6; 17:2-3, 11-12).

*Day 4*

D. As the house of God, the church is the dwelling place of God—the place where God can have His rest and put His trust (Eph. 2:22):

1. In this dwelling place God lives and moves to accomplish His will and to satisfy the desire of His heart (1:5, 9, 11; Phil. 2:13).

2. In the church as His dwelling place, God expresses Himself; all that He is and all that He is doing are expressed in the church (1 Cor. 3:16; 14:24-25).

3. The dwelling place of God is in our spirit; thus, our spirit is the place of His habitation (Eph. 2:22; Isa. 57:15; 66:1-2).

4. We need to grow in the divine life for the building up of God's house (1 Cor. 3:6, 16-17; Eph. 2:21; 4:15; 1 Pet. 2:2, 5).

*Day 5*

E. The church as the house of God—the Father's house—is the enlarged, universal, divine-human incorporation as the issue of Christ's being glorified by the Father with the divine glory (John 12:23; 13:31-32; 14:2):

1. The Father's house is for the processed and consummated Triune God to have a mutual abode with the believers in Christ (vv. 2-3, 23).

*Day 6*

2. The Father's house is for Christ, the embodiment of the processed Triune God, to make His home in our hearts (Eph. 3:16-17a).

3. The Father's house is for the invisible and mysterious Triune God to have a visible and solid household constituted by the

children of God, the species of God, with His divine life for their growth in life and for His rest, satisfaction, and manifestation (2:19; 1 Tim. 3:15).

F. The house of the living God is the genuine church in its divine nature and essential character, whereas the great house (2 Tim. 2:20) refers to the deteriorated church in its mixed character, as illustrated by the abnormally big tree in Matthew 13:31-32:

1. In the great house there are not only precious vessels but also base ones; hence, the great house cannot be the house of the living God (2 Tim. 2:20).

2. The great house is apostate Christendom, but the house of the living God is the genuine church of God—the household of God, the pillar and base of the truth, and the manifestation of God in the flesh (1 Tim. 3:15-16).

## Morning Nourishment

Acts  Take heed to yourselves and to all the flock, among
20:28  whom the Holy Spirit has placed you as overseers
to shepherd the church of God, which He obtained
through His own blood.

2 Cor.  But I, I will most gladly spend and be utterly spent
12:15  on behalf of your souls. If I love you more abundantly, am I loved less?

11:28  ...*There is this:* the crowd *of cares* pressing upon
me daily, the anxious concern for all the churches.

In Acts 20:28 Paul says that the church of God has been obtained "through His own blood." This indicates the precious love
of God for the church and the preciousness, the exceeding worth,
of the church in the eyes of God. Here the apostle does not touch
the divine life and nature of the church as in Ephesians 5:23-32,
but the value of the church as a treasure to God, a treasure which
He acquired with His own precious blood. Paul expected that the
elders as overseers would also treasure the church as God did.
(*Life-study of Acts*, p. 465)

## Today's Reading

The apostle Paul was a pattern of a lover of the church. The
church in Corinth spoke evil concerning Paul behind his back.
They said he was crafty in making gain, indemnifying himself by
sending Titus to receive the collection for the poor saints (2 Cor.
12:16). If the brothers in your locality were to say that you were
crafty and that you caught them by guile, you might want to leave
that locality. If you did leave, this would mean that you are not a
real lover of the church. Despite the Corinthians speaking such
an evil word about him, Paul still loved them. In 12:15 he said,
"But I, I will most gladly spend and be utterly spent on behalf of
your souls. If I love you more abundantly, am I loved less?" For
Paul to spend was to spend what he had, referring to his posses-
sions. For him to be spent was to spend what he was, referring to
his being. Paul was very frank, pure, and sincere, yet the church to

whom he ministered said that he was crafty. He was not happy with this, but he was not offended. He still loved the church.

The apostle Paul said that he was so glad to spend whatever he had and whatever he was. He loved the church to such an extent. If we do not love the church as the apostle Paul did, we actually have no position to talk about the church. If you are going to practice the church life and you do mean business with the Lord, you have to love the church with all that you have and with all that you are. You have to spend all that you have and all that you are on the church and for the church. May the Lord be gracious and merciful to us. If we mean business with the Lord in having a local expression of His Body, we cannot have it in a way of indifference. We should be able to tell the Lord that we love His Body more than ourselves. If you are this kind of person, you are in a position to talk about the church. We do not need theoretical teachings concerning the church, but we need the practical life of the church.

We should not be vain talkers concerning the church life, but we need to be involved in the practical life of the church. Do we really mean business to practice the church life on this earth today, or are we just talkers about some wonderful teachings concerning the church with no practicality? If we mean business with the Lord, we have to love the church with every drop of our blood. Paul was willing to spend and be spent on behalf of the church in Corinth in spite of the fact that the more he loved them, the less they loved him. This brother was a pattern as a lover of the church.

In 11:28 Paul refers to the "crowd of cares pressing upon me." Paul loved all the churches in all the different cities. He had a real care and a sincere anxiety for all of them. If we want 2 Corinthians to be our experience, we must be one with the church and love it unconditionally. (*An Autobiography of a Person in the Spirit*, pp. 67-69)

*Further Reading: Life-study of Acts,* msg. 53; *An Autobiography of a Person in the Spirit,* ch. 8

*Enlightenment and inspiration:* _____
_____
_____
_____

## Morning Nourishment

1 Tim.  ...The house of God, which is the church of the liv-
3:15-16  ing God....And confessedly, great is the mystery of
godliness: He who was manifested in the flesh...

Eph.  And He subjected all things under His feet and gave
1:22-23  Him *to be* Head over all things to the church, which
is His Body, the fullness of the One who fills all in all.

2:19  So then you are no longer strangers and sojourners,
but you are fellow citizens with the saints and
members of the household of God.

The church is also the house of God (1 Pet. 2:5). By this we do
not mean merely that the church is the dwelling of God. This
Greek word *oikos* means not only the house, the dwelling, but
also the household. *Oikos* means both house and also the folks,
the family, that make up the household; thus, it may also be
translated household (Eph. 2:19).

God's dwelling place today on earth is the church, and God, as
such a great Father, has a family, which is the church....We as the
church are God's house, God's dwelling place. At the same time,
we are God's family. Both the house of God and the family of God
are one entity, that is, a group of regenerated, called ones, indwelt
by God Himself. These called ones, who have been regenerated by
God with His life and who are being indwelt by this living God
with all that He is, are both God's dwelling place and His family.
This is more than an assembly. This is different from a group or
organization of people. This is something organic—organic in the
divine life, organic in the divine nature, and organic in the Triune
God. (*The Basic Revelation in the Holy Scriptures,* pp. 58-59)

## Today's Reading

The Body of Christ is the household of God (Eph. 2:19b). This
is the household of the faith—the universal family of God (Gal.
6:10), composed of God as the Father and the believers in Christ,
the many sons of God. God the Father has a great family of many
sons. The Father is God and the sons are "small gods" in life and
nature but not in the Godhead. If a father is a man, are not his

sons men? Since the father is a man, the sons all must be men. In the divine family, the Father is God, so all the sons are gods, the many God-men, in life and nature but not in the Godhead. First Timothy 3:15-16 reveals that the church is the manifestation of God in the flesh. (*The Practical Way to Live a Life according to the High Peak of the Divine Revelation in the Holy Scriptures,* p. 62)

Three verses which reveal that the church is the house of God are 1 Timothy 3:15; Hebrews 3:6; and 1 Peter 4:17. In 1 Timothy 3:15 Paul says, "If I delay...that you may know how one ought to conduct himself in the house of God, which is the church of the living God, the pillar and base of the truth."...Hebrews 3:6 refers to "Christ...as a Son over His house, whose house we are."...Today the house of God is the church.

The church has a twofold function. To Christ, the church is the Body; to God, the church is the house. Christ is the Head, and the church is the Body of the Head. This is one function of the church. God is the Father, and the church is His house. This is another function of the church. Just as Christ is the Head and the church is His Body, so God is the Father and the church is His house. The church as the Body of Christ is an organism. In like manner, the church as the house of God is a living entity, a living house.

First Peter 4:17...says, "For it is time for the judgment to begin from the house of God." Here we see that disciplinary judgment begins from God's own house. God's house, or household, is the church composed of the believers. From this house, as His own house, God begins His governmental administration by His disciplinary judgment over His own children, that He may have strong ground to judge, in His universal kingdom, those who are disobedient to His gospel and rebellious to His government. (*The Conclusion of the New Testament,* pp. 2227-2228)

*Further Reading: The Basic Revelation in the Holy Scriptures,* ch. 5; *The Practical Way to Live a Life according to the High Peak of the Divine Revelation in the Holy Scriptures,* ch. 6; *The Conclusion of the New Testament,* msg. 208

***Enlightenment and inspiration:*** _____

_____

_____

_____

### Morning Nourishment

John
17:2-3 Even as You have given Him authority over all flesh to give eternal life to all whom You have given Him. And this is eternal life, that they may know You, the only true God, and Him whom You have sent, Jesus Christ.

11 ...Holy Father, keep them in Your name, which You have given to Me, that they may be one even as We are.

1 Pet.
1:3 Blessed be the God and Father of our Lord Jesus Christ, who according to His great mercy has regenerated us unto a living hope through the resurrection of Jesus Christ from the dead.

The church is a composition of the believers, and the believers are children of God, born of Him and having His life and nature. Thus, they become members of the household of God.

In Ephesians 2:19 Paul says, "So then you are no longer strangers and sojourners, but you are fellow citizens with the saints and members of the household of God." Both the Jewish and the Gentile believers are members of God's household. God's household is a matter of life and enjoyment; all believers were born of God into His household to enjoy His riches. The members of God's family added together become the household of God, which is the house, the dwelling place, of God.

God's dwelling place is His household, His family, and His family comes into being by God's begetting. If we had not been begotten of God, God could not have a family. But God does have a great family, the largest family in the universe, composed of those who have been born of Him to be His children. Eventually, God's children will grow up to be His mature sons, and then they will become heirs. (*The Conclusion of the New Testament,* pp. 2231-2232)

### Today's Reading

In speaking of the church as the house of God, Paul specifically refers to God as the living God. The living God who lives in the church must be subjective to the church and not merely objective. The God who not only lives but also acts, moves, and works in His house, the church, is living. Because God is living, the church is also living in Him, by Him, and with Him. A living God and a living church live, move, and work together. The living church is the house of the living God. Therefore, in our meetings, service, and ministry we should give people the impression that the living God is living, moving, speaking, and acting among us.

The church, the house of the living God, is living in the Father's name and in the Father's life. This means that the church is living in the Father's reality. God's house is a living composition of His many children in the Father's life and reality. This means that where the house of God is, there is God the Father with His life and reality. This is similar to the church being the Body of Christ. Christ is not separate from the members of the Body, for, as the Head of the Body, Christ dwells in all the members. For this reason, Christ should not be counted as a separate member of the Body, because He is in all the members of the Body. The principle is the same with the church as God's house. The Father is not a separate member of the household, the house, but is in all the children.

The first characteristic of the status of the church is that it is an assembly called out of the world. The second characteristic is that the church is God's house composed of those who have been born of God. This second characteristic is a matter not merely of separation but of a spiritual, divine birth. In order to be the assembly, we need to be sanctified, that is, separated from the world. But to be a component of the house of God, we need to be born of God. Anyone who has not been born of God cannot be part of His house, part of His family. (*The Conclusion of the New Testament,* pp. 2228-2229)

*Further Reading: The Conclusion of the New Testament,* msg. 208; *A General Outline of God's Economy and the Proper Living of a God-man,* ch. 5

*Enlightenment and inspiration:* _____

_____

_____

_____

## Morning Nourishment

Eph.  In whom all the building, being fitted together, is
2:21-22  growing into a holy temple in the Lord; in whom you
also are being built together into a dwelling place of
God in spirit.
4:15  But holding to truth in love, we may grow up into
Him in all things, who is the Head, Christ.
1 Pet.  As newborn babes, long for the guileless milk of the
2:2  word in order that by it you may grow unto salvation.
5  You yourselves also, as living stones, are being built
up as a spiritual house...

Ephesians 2:22 tells us that God's dwelling place is in the believers' spirit,...the believers' regenerated human spirit indwelt
by God's Holy Spirit. God's Spirit is the Dweller, not the dwelling
place. The dwelling place is in the believers' spirit. God's Spirit
dwells in our regenerated spirit. Therefore, the dwelling place of
God is in our spirit. Our spirit is the place of God's habitation.
We all need to see clearly that God's dwelling place is in our
spirit, not in our heart or in our mind. Realizing that we have a
spirit and that God dwells in our regenerated spirit is crucial. If
we do not know how to exercise our spirit, it will be impossible for
us to understand anything concerning God's house, because this
house, the dwelling place of God, is in the believers' spirit. (*The
Conclusion of the New Testament*, p. 2230)

## Today's Reading

Because the church is God's dwelling place, the church is
where God expresses Himself....If you look at a person's house,
you will be able to tell what kind of person he is, because a person's house is his expression. The principle is the same with the
church as the dwelling place of God. In His house, His dwelling
place, God expresses Himself on earth....The church is God's
manifestation in the flesh [1 Tim. 3:15-16]. God not only desires to
make home in the church and to have a resting place there; He
also wants to express Himself in the church. He wants to practice
His New Testament economy, speak forth His desire, and

manifest His glory in the church. All that He is, all that He is doing, and all that He wants to obtain are to be manifested, expressed, in the church as His dwelling place.

The word "spiritual" in 1 Peter 2:5a denotes the qualification of the divine life that lives and grows (v. 2). The house of God subsists mainly by the divine life; hence, it is a spiritual house.

As believers in Christ, we need to grow and be transformed for the building up of God's spiritual house. God's goal in the believers is to have a house built up with spiritual stones, not separated and scattered stones, not even a pile of stones merely gathered together, but stones built up with one another. Hence, feeding on Christ by the nourishing milk in the word of God (vv. 2-3) is not only for growing in life but also for building up. Growing is for building up. Although the nourishing milk of the word is for the soul through the mind, it eventually nourishes our spirit, making us not soulish but spiritual, suitable for building up a spiritual house for God.

We would emphasize the fact that the church is not only the assembly of God but also the household of God. The church is not only something separated from the world but something born of God, regenerated by Him. God does not simply separate sinners from the world and put them together to be His household. In addition to separation, there must be a change of life and nature through regeneration. For this reason, after God separated us from the world, He put Himself into us, germinating us, begetting us as His children. It is in this way that we have become His household. This household then becomes God's house, His dwelling place in our spirit. Intrinsically speaking, therefore, the church as God's household is in our God-created, God-regenerated, and God-indwelt spirit. It is crucial for us to see this. (*The Conclusion of the New Testament*, pp. 2229-2232)

*Further Reading: The Conclusion of the New Testament*, msg. 208;
*Four Crucial Elements of the Bible—Christ, the Spirit, Life, and the Church*, ch. 10; *The Satanic Chaos in the Old Creation and the Divine Economy for the New Creation*, ch. 4

*Enlightenment and inspiration:* _____

_____

_____

_____

## *Morning Nourishment*

John
14:2
In My Father's house are many abodes; if *it were not so,* I would have told you; for I go to prepare a place for you.

23 Jesus answered and said to him, If anyone loves Me, he will keep My word, and My Father will love him, and We will come to him and make an abode with him.

Eph.
2:19-20
...You are fellow citizens with the saints and members of the household of God, being built upon the foundation of the apostles and prophets, Christ Jesus Himself being the cornerstone.

3:16-17 That He would grant you, according to the riches of His glory, to be strengthened with power through His Spirit into the inner man, that Christ may make His home in your hearts through faith...

The Father's house is a divine and human incorporation of the processed and consummated God constituted with His redeemed, regenerated, and transformed elect. The Father's house is not only a constitution—it is an incorporation....In John 14:2a the Lord Jesus said, "In My Father's house are many abodes." All the believers in Christ, redeemed through His blood, regenerated with His life by His Spirit, and transformed with the divine element by the life-giving Spirit, are the "abodes" in the Father's house. In our houses we have rooms. As believers in Christ and members of the Body of Christ, we all are rooms, abodes, in the Father's house. (*The Issue of Christ Being Glorified by the Father with the Divine Glory,* pp. 32-33)

## *Today's Reading*

The Father's house is built up by the constant visitation to the redeemed elect of the Father and the Son with the Spirit who indwells the redeemed elect to be the mutual dwelling place of the consummated Triune God and His redeemed elect. In John 14:23 the Lord Jesus said, "If anyone loves Me, he will keep My word, and My Father will love him, and We will come to him and make an abode with him." Verse 2 tells us that in the Father's house there are many abodes, and in verse 23 we see that these abodes are built up by the Father and the Son's visitation to those who love Him. The Spirit is not explicitly mentioned in verse 23 but rather is implied, for the Spirit dwells in the regenerated spirit of all those who love the Lord Jesus.

From our experience we know that the Father and the Son pay us a constant visitation. In our daily life the Father and the Son often come to visit us. We may be at home, at school, or at work, but wherever we may be the Father and the Son come to visit us to do a building work in us, making an abode which will be a mutual dwelling place for the Triune God and for us. This is the building up of the Father's house through the constant visitation of the Triune God.

The Father's house is built upon the foundation of the apostles and prophets with Christ as the cornerstone, and it is growing into the holy temple of the Lord, the dwelling place of God in the believers' spirit (Eph. 2:19-22)....In this building Christ is making His home in the hearts of the believers strengthened in their inner man by the Father according to the riches of His glory with power through His Spirit unto the fullness (the expression) of the consummated Triune God (Eph. 3:16-19).

The Father's house is both the household of God and the kingdom of God....As the household of God the Father's house is constituted by the children of God, the species of God, with His divine life for their growth in life and for His manifestation (Eph. 2:19). This life is for our growth in life and also for God's manifestation....The Father's house is also the kingdom of God, which is composed of the believers in Christ as the citizens (John 3:3, 5; Rev. 1:4, 6; Eph. 2:19; Matt. 16:18-19; Acts 1:3; 28:31). (*The Issue of Christ Being Glorified by the Father with the Divine Glory*, pp. 33-34)

*Further Reading: The Issue of Christ Being Glorified by the Father with the Divine Glory*, chs. 4, 6

*Enlightenment and inspiration:* _____

_____

_____

_____

## Morning Nourishment

John
14:2
In My Father's house are many abodes; if *it were* not *so,* I would have told you; for I go to prepare a place for you.

1 Tim.
3:15
But if I delay, *I write* that you may know how one ought to conduct himself in the house of God, which is the church of the living God, the pillar and base of the truth.

2 Tim.
2:20
But in a great house there are not only gold and silver vessels but also wooden and earthen; and some are unto honor, and some unto dishonor.

The Father's house for His dwelling (John 14:2) refers to the divine family with the children born of God (1:12-13) and to Bethel (the house of God) as the place for the heavenly ladder to bring heaven to earth and join earth to heaven (1:51). The Father's house is also the temple of God as the house of God, which was Christ Himself before His resurrection and was enlarged with His believers through His resurrection (2:16-22). Furthermore, the Father's house is a mutual abode for the Triune God and the believers built up by the Father and the Son (14:23), consummating in the New Jerusalem (Rev. 21). The Spirit indwells this abode with the Father and the Son for the mutual dwelling place of the Triune God and His transformed elect. (*Crystallization-study of the Gospel of John,* p. 112)

## Today's Reading

The recovery of the church also requires that we cleanse ourselves from the vessels unto dishonor in the great house—the apostate Christendom. "In a great house there are not only gold and silver vessels but also wooden and earthen; and some are unto honor, and some unto dishonor. If therefore anyone cleanses himself from these, he will be a vessel unto honor, sanctified, useful to the master, prepared unto every good work" (2 Tim. 2:20-21). Here Paul uses the expression "a great house." The house of God defined in 1 Timothy 3:15 and 16 is the genuine church in its divine nature and essential character as the foundation of the truth, whereas the great house here refers to the deteriorated church in its mixed character, as illustrated by the abnormally big tree in Matthew 13:31-32. In this great house there are not only precious vessels but also base ones. For this reason, we cannot believe that the great house in 2 Timothy 2:20 refers to the church as the house of the living God in 1 Timothy 3:15. The great house is certainly not the house of the living God, which is the great mystery of godliness and also God manifest in the flesh. Such a house cannot contain vessels unto dishonor. Hence, the great house must refer to Christendom. Furthermore, this great house is equal to the big tree in Matthew 13. The genuine church today is the house of the living God, whereas the apostate Christendom is the great house. Just as many unclean birds lodge in the big tree, so in the great house there are vessels unto dishonor, wooden and earthen vessels. In the genuine church, however, there are only gold and silver vessels.

Honorable vessels are of both the divine nature (gold) and the redeemed and regenerated human nature (silver). These are the genuine believers. Dishonorable vessels are of the fallen human nature (wooden and earthen) and signify the false believers. The word "these" in 2 Timothy 2:21 indicates that the genuine believers need to cleanse themselves from the dishonorable vessels. This means that we must stay away from them. If we cleanse ourselves from negative things and negative persons, we shall be vessels unto honor, sanctified, useful to the master and prepared unto every good work. (*The Conclusion of the New Testament,* pp. 2458-2459)

*Further Reading: Crystallization-study of the Gospel of John,* msg. 11; *The Conclusion of the New Testament,* msg. 231

***Enlightenment and inspiration:*** _____

_____
_____
_____

### *Hymns*, #852

1    Thy dwelling-place, O Lord, I love;
      It is Thy church so blessed,
      It is Thy joy and heart's delight
      And where Thy heart finds rest.

2    For her, Thyself Thou gavest, Lord,
      That she be Thine, complete;
      For her, I too my body give,
      Thy heart's desire to meet.

3    For her, Thou hast become my life,
      That she my living be;
      For her, I would forsake myself,
      That she be filled with Thee.

4    The church is Thy beloved Bride,
      Thou in Thy Body seen;
      She is my joy and heart's desire,
      The one on whom I lean.

5    In her, Thy full supply, O Lord,
      Thou dost to me impart;
      In her am I possessed by Thee
      To satisfy Thy heart.

6    Thy dwelling-place, O Lord, I love;
      It is Thy church, Thy home;
      In it I would forever live
      And never longer roam.

*Composition for prophecy with main point and
sub-points:* _____

_____

_____

_____

_____

_____

_____

_____

_____

_____

_____

_____

_____

_____

_____

_____

_____

_____

_____

_____

_____

_____

_____

_____

_____

_____

_____

_____

_____

_____

_____

_____

_____

_____

_____

## The Function of the Church (2)
## The Pillar and Base of the Truth

Scripture Reading: 1 Tim. 3:15; 2:4; 2 Tim. 2:15, 25; Titus 1:1, 14

*Day 1*    I. As used in 1 and 2 Timothy and Titus, *truth* denotes the contents of God's New Testament economy (1 Tim. 1:4; 3:15; 2:4; 2 Tim. 2:15, 25; Titus 1:1, 14).

II. The Lord wants His church to know Him as the truth and to receive and enjoy Him as life (1 John 1:1-2, 5-6; John 11:25; 14:6; 18:37b):

A. *Truth* means reality, denoting all the real things revealed in God's Word, which are mainly Christ as the embodiment of God and the church as the Body of Christ (1 Tim. 2:4; Col. 2:9, 19):

1. The foundation in 2 Timothy 2:19 is the church as the foundation of the truth; this corresponds with the base of the truth, which holds the truth, especially the truth of the resurrection of Christ (1 Tim. 3:15; Acts 4:33).

2. Because the Lord's recovery has the firm foundation of the truth, it is not hurt by any attack (2 Tim. 2:19).

B. The church is built with the divine life in Christ, a life which is indestructible, unconquerable, and able to withstand decline into death from any source (1 Tim. 1:16; 6:12, 19; 2 Tim. 1:1, 10; Titus 1:2; 3:7):

1. The church is the firm foundation of God standing in the eternal life (2 Tim. 2:19).

2. The Lord's recovery is protected by the unconquerable divine life (Heb. 7:16; Acts 2:24):

a. The recovery is built on something eternal and divine—God's life with its nature (John 3:15; 2 Pet. 1:4).

        b. For this reason, not even the gates of Hades can conquer the Lord's recovery (Matt. 16:18; Rev. 1:18).

C. Both the truth and the life are Christ Himself (John 14:6):

    1. Life is the inward and intrinsic content, and truth is the outward definition and explanation (1:4; 18:37b; 8:12, 32, 36; 17:17).

    2. The experience of the Lord as life is contained in the Lord as the truth:

        a. If we are not clear about the truth and do not understand and know the truth, we will have no way to enjoy Christ as our life (Col. 1:5-6; 3:4).

        b. In order to experience the Lord as life, we must know the truth (John 14:6; 11:25; 8:32, 36).

D. The content of the church must be the growth of Christ in us as truth and life (Col. 2:19; 3:4):

    1. Truth is the shining, the expression, of the divine light (John 8:12, 32, 36).

    2. The standard of the truth should constantly be raised higher among all the churches in the Lord's recovery (1 Tim. 2:4; 3:15).

    3. We need to grow in life, be saved in life, be filled with life, and reign in life (Eph. 4:13-16; Rom. 5:10, 17).

E. By life and truth Paul encouraged Timothy and inoculated him against the decline of the church (2 Tim. 1:1, 10; 2:15, 25):

    1. Though the churches may become degraded and many of the saints may backslide in unfaithfulness, the eternal life remains forever the same (1:1, 10).

    2. The word of the truth, rightly unfolded, enlightens the darkened people, inoculates against the poison, swallows up the death, and brings the distracted back to the proper track (2:15, 25).

*Day 4*   **III. The church is the supporting pillar and the holding base of the truth (1 Tim. 3:15):**

A. The truth is the Triune God, having Christ as the embodiment, center, and expression, to produce the church as the Body of Christ, the house of God, and the kingdom of God (Col. 2:9; Eph. 1:22-23; 4:16; 1 Tim. 3:15; John 3:3, 5).

B. *Truth* in 1 Timothy 3:15 refers to the real things revealed in the New Testament concerning Christ and the church according to God's New Testament economy (Matt. 16:16, 18; Eph. 5:32):

1. The church is the supporting pillar and holding base of these realities.

2. A local church should be such a building that holds, bears, and testifies the truth, the reality, of Christ and the church.

C. The church bears Christ as the reality; the church testifies to the whole universe that Christ, and Christ alone, is the reality (John 1:14, 17; 14:6).

D. God's New Testament economy is composed of two mysteries: Christ as the mystery of God and the church as the mystery of Christ (Col. 2:2; Eph. 3:4):

1. Christ and the church, the Head and the Body, are the contents of the reality of God's New Testament economy (Col. 1:18; 2:19).

2. As the pillar which bears the truth and the base which upholds the pillar, the church testifies the reality, the truth, of Christ as the mystery of God and the church as the mystery of Christ.

*Day 5*   **IV. In the church life, we all need to come to the full knowledge of the truth (1 Tim. 2:4; 4:3; 2 Tim. 2:25; 3:7; Titus 1:1):**

A. Every saved person should have a full knowledge, a complete realization, of the real things revealed in God's Word (1 John 2:21).

B. The full knowledge of the truth is a thorough

apprehension of the truth, a full acknowledg-
ment and appreciation of the reality of all the
spiritual and divine things that we have
received through faith (1 Tim. 2:4; 4:3; 2 Tim.
2:25).

C. The present truth is the truth that is present
with the believers, which they have already
received and now possess (2 Pet. 1:12).

D. To cut straight the word of the truth is to unfold
without bias or distortion the reality of God's
economy revealed in the New Testament (2 Tim.
2:15).

*Day 6*

E. For God's purpose, we must stand firm for the
full knowledge of the truth and fight the good
fight against the powers of darkness (1 Tim.
6:12; 2 Tim. 4:7).

F. The kind of church we build up depends on the
kind of truth we teach; thus, there is the desperate need of the living truth to produce the
church, to help the church to exist, and to build
up the church (1 Tim. 3:15).

## Morning Nourishment

1 Tim.   ...*I write* that you may know how one ought to con-
3:15     duct himself in the house of God, which is the church
         of the living God, the pillar and base of the truth.

2 Tim.   However the firm foundation of God stands, having
2:19     this seal, The Lord knows those who are His, and, Let
         everyone who names the name of the Lord depart
         from unrighteousness.

Rev.     And the living One; and I became dead, and behold, I
1:18     am living forever and ever; and I have the keys of
         death and of Hades.

Matt.    And I also say to you that you are Peter, and upon this
16:18    rock I will build My church, and the gates of Hades
         shall not prevail against it.

Many Christian teachers claim that the foundation in 2 Timothy 2:19 refers to Christ. It is true that in 1 Corinthians 3:11 Paul says that Christ is the unique foundation. Apart from Him, we do not have any other foundation. Nevertheless, if we consider verse 19 according to the context of the chapter, we shall see that the foundation here does not refer to Christ as the foundation of the church, but refers to the church as the foundation, or base, of the truth. Verses 14 through 18 give instruction concerning how to deal with heresies on the negative side and how to handle the truth on the positive side. According to the context of verses 15, 18, and 25, the foundation here does not refer to Christ as the foundation of the church, but to the church as the foundation of the truth. This corresponds to "the base of the truth," which holds the truth (1 Tim. 3:15), especially the truth of the resurrection of Christ (Acts 4:33).

The church is built with the divine life in Christ, a life which is indestructible, unconquerable (Heb. 7:16; Acts 2:24), and able to withstand decline into death from any source. Hence, the church is the firm foundation of God that stands forever against any heresy. No matter what kind of heresies may come in or how extensively the gangrene may spread, this firm foundation stands. (*Life-study of 2 Timothy,* pp. 31-32)

## Today's Reading

Certain of those who left the Lord's recovery expected that soon afterwards the recovery would collapse. However, because it is built upon a firm foundation, the recovery did not collapse and it will never collapse. Had the Lord's recovery been founded on something other than the divine life, the eternal life, it would have collapsed long ago. But because the recovery has the firm foundation of the truth, it is not hurt by attack. On the contrary, those who seek to damage the recovery actually damage themselves, and at the same time they strengthen the recovery and expose the firmness of its foundation. The recovery is built on something eternal and divine—God's life with His nature. For this reason, not even the gates of Hades can conquer it. Because it is built on the indestructible and unconquerable eternal life, the firm foundation of the truth stands. In recent years, it has not been necessary for us to protect the Lord's recovery. It has been protected by the unconquerable divine life. Hence, the church is the firm foundation of God standing in the eternal life.

Paul says that this firm foundation has "this seal." The seal has two sides. On the Lord's side it is: "The Lord knows those who are His." This is based on the Lord's divine life, which He has given to all His believers and which has brought them into an organic union with Him, making them one with Him and causing them to become His. On our side it is: "Let everyone who names the name of the Lord depart from unrighteousness." This is the issue of the divine life: it enables us to depart from unrighteousness and keeps us blameless in His holy name. The church as the firm foundation in the divine life bears such a two-sided seal, testifying that the Lord's divine life has made us His and has kept us from things which are contrary to His righteous way. (*Life-study of 2 Timothy,* pp. 32-33)

*Further Reading: Life-study of 2 Timothy,* msg. 4

***Enlightenment and inspiration:*** _____

_____

_____

_____

## *Morning Nourishment*

John    Jesus said to him, I am the way and the reality and the
14:6    life; no one comes to the Father except through Me.
1:4     In Him was life, and the life was the light of men.
8:32    And you shall know the truth, and the truth shall set
        you free.
17:17   Sanctify them in the truth; Your word is truth.

The Lord's recovery is mainly founded upon four pillars: the truth, life, the church, and the gospel. The reason Christianity is degraded is that it has lost the truth and is short of life. The Bible tells us that the Lord Himself is the truth and the life. In John 14:6 the Lord Jesus said, "I am the way and the reality and the life." In this verse the reality is the truth. Thus, the Lord said that He Himself is the life and the truth.

Both the truth and the life are the Lord Himself, but they are two different aspects of what He is. The difference is that the truth is an outward definition and explanation, and life is the inward and intrinsic content. The Lord is in us as our life, but the experience of life needs an explanation. This explanation is the truth. If we receive the Lord according to this explanation, we have life. Hence, in order to experience and enjoy the Lord as life, we must know the truth. The experience of the Lord as life is contained in the Lord as the truth. If we are not clear about the truth and do not understand or know the truth, we will have no way to enjoy the Lord as our life. For this reason we must spend an adequate amount of time to learn the truth. (*Truth, Life, the Church, and the Gospel—the Four Great Pillars in the Lord's Recovery*, p. 69)

## *Today's Reading*

The Lord has not left us in darkness. Today all of His truths are contained in the Bible, which He has given to us. We must realize that the Bible is a book of life. The reason the Bible is a book of life is that its entire content is truth. All experienced Christians confess that no one can enjoy Christ as life if he does not know the Bible or understand the truth in the Bible. We need to go to the supermarkets to buy food for our physical body to be fed and

sustained. In like manner, we must come to the Bible to receive
the truth that is in it if we want to receive and enjoy the Lord as
life. All the truths in the Bible are food for our spiritual life.

The Bible is not merely a book of knowledge. All the knowledge contained in the Bible is in fact truth, and in this truth, life is
concealed. When we read the Bible, if we study only the letter, but
not the intrinsic truth within, we will not receive life. Hence, every Bible reader has to see the truth that is conveyed through the
letter of the Word. Once we see the truth, we will spontaneously
touch life. The life-studies have been published to help us enter
into the depths of the letter of the Word. Therefore, all those who
carefully study the life-studies will surely gain a certain amount
of experience. The life-studies bring us into the biblical truths,
from which we may receive the genuine life supply.

Today the Lord's recovery is a recovery of the truth and of life.
We all know that the decline of Christianity is due to the fact that
it has lost both the truth and life. This loss of the truth and life
eventually produced many human methods and worldly organi-
zations, which are not what the Lord wants....Instead, He wants
His church to know Him as the truth and to receive and enjoy
Him as life. The entire content of the church must be the growth
of Christ in us as truth and life. This may be likened to an orchard,
the entire content of which is the fruits of life produced from the
fruit trees. In an orchard we cannot find any organization or be-
havior. We can only see the fruit trees growing and bearing fruit
as the issue of their growth in life. This should be the situation of
the churches in the Lord's recovery today. In the churches we do
not want to have any organization or human methods. Rather, we
want to minister to God's people for their growth by planting and
watering as the apostle Paul said in 1 Corinthians 3:6 and 9.
(*Truth, Life, the Church, and the Gospel—the Four Great Pillars
in the Lord's Recovery,* pp. 69-71)

*Further Reading: Truth, Life, the Church, and the Gospel—the Four
Great Pillars in the Lord's Recovery,* chs. 4-7

***Enlightenment and inspiration:*** _____
_____
_____
_____

## Morning Nourishment

John    Again therefore Jesus spoke to them, saying, I am
8:12    the light of the world; he who follows Me shall by
        no means walk in darkness, but shall have the
        light of life.

32      And you shall know the truth, and the truth shall
        set you free.

36      If therefore the Son sets you free, you shall be free
        indeed.

Truth is the expression of light....Whenever light shines,
we receive truth. Light shines in darkness. In 1 and 2 Timothy, two books dealing with degradation, truth is mentioned
often because during a period of darkness there is the need for
the shining of the light, the expression of the light.

Truth is the shining of light. Wherever there is light, there
is God, for God is light (1 John 1:5). When the light shines upon
us, it becomes the truth. In Romans 8 Paul encourages us to
walk according to the spirit, but in John's second and third
Epistles, also written in a time of degradation, John speaks of
walking in the truth. Although in his other writings John em-
phasized life, in these two Epistles he spoke much about the
truth. For example, in 3 John 4 he says, "I have no greater joy
than these things, that I hear that my children are walking in
the truth." Whenever we are in a time of degradation and darkness, we need the shining of the light so that we may know how
to walk in the proper way. (*Truth Messages*, pp. 8-9)

## Today's Reading

Truth is not merely a report, not simply words written in
the Bible; it is a heavenly, spiritual vision televised into our
being. We all need to learn to differentiate the speaking that
gives merely a news report from the speaking that televises a
vision into us. Most of the sermons preached in the so-called
churches today are like newspaper reports. Because many
preachers use the Bible like a newspaper, there is very little of
the heavenly vision.

Because we all need to see the heavenly vision, in Ephesians 1 Paul prayed that we would have a spirit of wisdom and revelation. Actually, such a spirit is simply the vision televised into our being by the Spirit.

According to the Bible, the Spirit is called the Spirit of truth, the Spirit of reality (John 14:17). The Spirit of reality is the heavenly electricity by which spiritual things are televised into our being. The Bible also says that the Word is truth (John 17:17). All the spiritual facts are contained in the Word and conveyed by it....However, without the enlightenment from the divine electricity, these facts are mere doctrines. But when the Spirit shines upon these facts recorded and conveyed in the Bible, they become truth, reality.

Christ, His person, His redemptive work, and all His accomplishments are facts contained in and conveyed by the Word. The Spirit seeks the opportunity to shine upon the Word. When He does so, we receive the truth. In knowing the truth, we thus have the facts, the Word, and the Spirit. The incarnation, crucifixion, resurrection, and ascension have all been accomplished. The wonderful Christ who is God and man is now the life-giving Spirit. These are facts, and not even Satan can deny them. We have not only the facts, but the fact-conveying Word. Furthermore, we have the Spirit. If we have the Word without the Spirit, we shall not have the vision. This means that we shall not have the truth, because the truth comes only when the Spirit shines. If we read the Word without the shining of the Spirit, we may have doctrine or news reports, but not the truth, the reality, or the vision. Thank the Lord that the shining Spirit is always within us. Whenever we open ourselves to Him, the light shines. As the light shines on the Word, certain things stand out and make a deep impression upon us. This is the truth, the vision transmitted by the heavenly television. (*Truth Messages*, pp. 17-20)

*Further Reading: Truth Messages*, chs. 1-3

***Enlightenment and inspiration:*** _____

_____

_____

_____

## Morning Nourishment

1 Tim.  ...The house of God, which is the church of the living
3:15   God, the pillar and base of the truth.
Matt.  And Simon Peter answered and said, You are the
16:16  Christ, the Son of the living God.
   18  And I also say to you that you are Peter, and upon
       this rock I will build My church, and the gates of
       Hades shall not prevail against it.
Eph.   This mystery is great, but I speak with regard to
5:32   Christ and the church.

The church as the house of God is also the pillar and base of
the truth. As the pillar, the church supports the truth, and as the
base, the church holds the truth. The truth is the Triune God with
Christ as the embodiment, as the center, and as the image to produce the church to be the organism as Christ's Body, as God's
home, and as God's kingdom. Anything else is not the truth, and
to teach anything else is to teach differently. Doctrines such as
head covering, foot-washing, and methods of baptism are doctrines, but not the truth, which we need to teach. The truth is just
one thing—the Triune God, having Christ as the center, the embodiment, the image, and the expression, to produce the church
as the Body of Christ, the house of God, and the kingdom of God.
We are one in this truth. We are not one in the different small
points in the Bible. (*The Satanic Chaos in the Old Creation and
the Divine Economy for the New Creation*, p. 105)

## Today's Reading

In 1 Timothy 3:15 Paul tells us that the church as the house
of the living God is "the pillar and base of the truth." The church
is the supporting pillar and holding base of the truth. Here truth
refers to the real things revealed in the New Testament concerning Christ and the church according to God's New Testament economy. The church is the supporting pillar and holding
base of these realities. A local church should be such a building
that holds, bears, and testifies the truth, the reality, of Christ
and the church.

God's New Testament economy is composed of two mysteries: Christ as the mystery of God (Col. 2:2) and the church as the mystery of Christ (Eph. 3:4). Christ and the church, the Head and the Body, are the contents of the reality of God's New Testament economy. As the pillar which bears the truth and the base which upholds the pillar, the church testifies the reality, the truth, of Christ as the mystery of God and the church as the mystery of Christ.

According to the context, we may say that the truth in 1 Timothy 3:15 denotes the mystery of godliness, the manifestation of God in the flesh, in verse 16. The unique truth, the unique reality, in the universe is the manifestation of the Triune God in the flesh. As we shall now see, this manifestation is not only in Christ but also in the church. (*The Conclusion of the New Testament,* pp. 2232-2233)

In 1 Timothy 3:15 the apostle Paul says that the church is not only the pillar of the truth, but also the base of the truth (Gk.). A pillar, which is a standing column, needs a solid base. The Greek word for "base" in this verse actually means a bulwark, a solid structure that upholds the pillar. As the pillar of the truth, the church must also have a solid base, a strong bulwark. A bulwark affords protection and defense, especially during a time of war. The church must be so solid in the truth that it will be a bulwark of the truth during times of fighting. This bulwark should be so solid that nothing, not even the "bombs" of the enemy, can shake it. The pillar rests upon such a bulwark. In order to be the pillar and base of the truth, we all must be solid, strong, clear, and rich in the truth. Every local church must be a solid bulwark and a high pillar. In every locality the pillar must be built up higher and higher to testify the truth to the whole universe. (*Truth Messages,* pp. 22-23)

*Further Reading: The Satanic Chaos in the Old Creation and the Divine Economy for the New Creation, ch. 4; The Conclusion of the New Testament, msg. 208; Truth Messages, chs. 1-2*

***Enlightenment and inspiration:*** _____

_____

_____
_____

## *Morning Nourishment*

2 Tim.  **Be diligent to present yourself approved to God,**
2:15  **an unashamed workman, cutting straight the word of the truth.**

25  **In meekness correcting those who oppose, if perhaps God may give them repentance unto the full knowledge of the truth.**

Titus  **Paul, a slave of God and an apostle of Jesus Christ**
1:1  **according to the faith of God's chosen ones and the full knowledge of the truth, which is according to godliness.**

In 2 Timothy 2:15...Paul indicates that the inoculator is to be a workman. As a carpenter, this workman must cut straight the word of the truth. This means to unfold the word of God in its various parts rightly and straightly without distortion. Just as a carpenter has the skill to cut wood in a straight way, so the Lord's workman needs the skill to cut straight the word of truth. This is necessary because in the decline of the church so many truths are twisted and presented in a warped, biased form. (*Life-study of 2 Timothy,* pp. 26-27)

## *Today's Reading*

Among Christians today, only the superficial aspects of the truth are not twisted. Virtually all the deeper things of the truth have been distorted. Concerning these things, many have not cut the word of truth straightly, but cut it in a way that is curved and biased. Therefore, we should be not only teachers, soldiers, contenders, and farmers, but also workmen, carpenters, cutting straight the word of the truth. The truth here does not merely denote biblical doctrine; it refers to the contents and the reality of God's New Testament economy. The main elements of this truth are Christ as the mystery of God and the embodiment of God and the church as the mystery of Christ and the Body of Christ. We all need to learn to cut straight the word of truth with respect to Christ and the church.

Certain of the Brethren teachers interpret Paul's word about cutting straight the word of truth to mean dividing the Bible into various dispensations: innocence, conscience, human government, promise, law, grace, and kingdom. The Bible can be understood according to these dispensations. However, arranging the Word into dispensations is not what Paul means in 2:15 about cutting straight the word of the truth. As used in the three books of 1 and 2 Timothy and Titus, the word truth has a specific significance: it denotes the contents of God's New Testament economy. Not realizing this, many readers of the Bible think that in 2:15 Paul is speaking of truth in a general way. But we need to understand the word truth in this verse according to its usage in the three books of 1 and 2 Timothy and Titus. First Timothy 3:15 says that the church is "the pillar and base of the truth." This truth is the mystery of godliness, God manifest in the flesh. The church should bear, uphold, this truth, this reality. Numerous times in these three Epistles Paul speaks of the truth. For example, in 1 Timothy 2:4 he says that God "desires all men to be saved and to come to the full knowledge of the truth." The word of the truth in 2 Timothy 2:15 refers to the healthy words of God's New Testament economy. As workmen, we should learn not merely to divide the Bible into dispensations. This is too superficial. We must learn to unfold the word of the truth concerning God's economy. If we would do this, we need to consider carefully Paul's use of the word truth in these three Epistles. If we consider these books carefully, we shall see that truth here denotes the reality of the contents of the New Testament economy of God. Therefore, to cut straight the word of the truth is to unfold without bias or distortion the reality of God's economy revealed in the New Testament. (*Life-study of 2 Timothy,* pp. 27-28)

*Further Reading: Life-study of 2 Timothy,* msg. 3

***Enlightenment and inspiration:*** _____

_____

_____

_____

### Morning Nourishment

1 Cor.   But in the church I would rather speak five words
14:19-20  with my mind, that I might instruct others also, than
          ten thousand words in a tongue. Brothers, do not be
          children in *your* understanding, but in malice be
          babes and in your understanding be full-grown.
1 Tim.    Who desires all men to be saved and to come to the
2:4       full knowledge of the truth.
3:15      ...*I write* that you may know how one ought to con-
          duct himself in the house of God, which is the church
          of the living God, the pillar and base of the truth.

We should encourage the saints to have a private time in the
Lord's Word and that they should do this as a proper rule of
their daily life. Regardless of how busy or how tired we are, we
can reserve thirty minutes a day for a time with the Lord in the
Word. It all depends upon our will. If there is the will, there is the
way. To save half an hour among twenty-four hours is not a hard
thing. If the saints could practice one hour or more in the Lord's
Word this would be wonderful, but at least we should encourage
them to give a half an hour to the Lord every day. The saints
should be encouraged to separate or sanctify thirty minutes
every day to the Lord. We all can realize what a blessing this
will be, and I believe this will make the Lord very pleased. Then
every local church needs to find a way to carry out the meetings
in the principle of giving the saints the proper education in the
full knowledge of the truth. (*Elders' Training, Book 3: The Way to
Carry Out the Vision,* pp. 146-147)

### Today's Reading

History has clearly shown us that the existence of a denomi-
nation, free group, or the genuine church life all depends on the
doctrines. If there are no doctrines, there is no church. Since the
Lord's recovery has come to the United States, we have stressed
very much that the building up of the church depends upon the
experience of Christ, upon the life-giving Spirit, and upon the
matters of life. Seemingly, I am saying something different

now....The so-called "Spirit" cannot build up the church, but the solid truth or the solid doctrines can. Certainly, what kind of church you will build up depends upon what kind of truth you teach....We have stressed greatly that the churches are built up not by mere doctrines but by Christ, by the Spirit, and by life. Since 1962 a great many messages have been put out on the truth. If we had not put out any messages on the truth since the recovery came to this country and we had merely learned to pray and to exercise in the gifts such as tongues and healings, today's situation would be very poor. In the past, we practiced in this way for a short time, and we found out that the issue was poor....We fully realized that to produce the church, to have the church exist, and to build up the church we needed to put out the solid, living truths full of Christ, full of the Spirit, and full of life. God's way to carry out His economy is to use His holy Word.

Suppose that...we had not had a Bible in our hands during the past 2,000 years since the Lord Jesus resurrected and ascended to the heavens; everything would be in the air and nothing could be solid. Even the things concerning the Spirit could not be solid. The Spirit depends upon the Word. This is why the Lord said that the words that He spoke to us are spirit (John 6:63). The words which the Lord speaks are the solid spirit. Without the Word the Spirit is not so solid....Today, however, we have the Bible. In innumerable instances we have seen that whenever people contact the holy Word, many times they get the Spirit, but it is hard to give an instance where people touch the Spirit and then they get the Word....A principle has been set up through history that there is the desperate need of the living truth to produce the church, to help the church exist, and to build up the church. (*Elders' Training, Book 3: The Way to Carry Out the Vision,* pp. 101-103)

*Further Reading: Elders' Training, Book 3: The Way to Carry Out the Vision,* chs. 1, 9-11, 13; *Life-study of 1 Timothy,* msg. 3; *Life-study of Titus,* msg. 2

***Enlightenment and inspiration:*** _____

_____

_____

_____

## *Hymns,* #801

1    O living Word of God, God's image true,
     Thou art the content of God's written word;
     God in Thee we have met, God's fulness found,
     And in the Scripture we Thyself have heard.


2    No man has e'er seen God, apart from Thee,
     Without the Scripture Thee we'd hardly see;
     Thou to the human race God hast declared,
     And thru the Scripture Thou art shown to me.


3    Perfect embodiment Thou art of God,
     A portrait full the Scripture gives of Thee;
     In Thee we comprehend God's image true,
     And thru the Scripture Thou art real to me.


4    Life-giving Spirit Thou, as well as Word,
     Now e'en the Spirit in the Word Thou art;
     When thru the Spirit giv'n, I touch the Word,
     Fulness divine to me Thou dost impart.


5    In Thee I may with God have fellowship,
     And thru the Scripture I on Thee may feed;
     Thru study of the Word with prayer to God
     Thy glorious riches fully meet my need.


6    Teach me to exercise my spirit, Lord,
     Thy Word to study, so to contact Thee,
     That Thou, the living Word, with Scripture, too,
     As one my daily manna e'er may be.

*Composition for prophecy with main point and sub-points:* _____

_____

_____

_____

_____

_____

_____

_____

_____

_____

_____

_____

_____

_____

_____

_____

_____

_____

_____

_____

_____

_____

_____

_____

_____

_____

_____

_____

_____

_____

_____

_____

_____

_____

_____

_____

_____

_____

_____

_____

### The Function of the Church (3)
### The Manifestation of God in the Flesh

Scripture Reading: 1 Tim. 3:15-16; John 1:1, 14; Col. 2:9;
Rev. 21:2, 10-11

Day 1
&
Day 2
I. God's good pleasure, the desire of His heart, is
to have many sons for the expression of His
Son so that He may be expressed in the Son
through the Spirit and in the Body, which con-
summates in the New Jerusalem (Eph. 1:5, 9;
3:19b, 21; Rom. 8:29).

II. God's manifestation was first in Christ as an
individual expression in the flesh (1 Tim. 3:16;
Col. 2:9; John 1:1, 14):

A. The New Testament does not say that the Son of
God was incarnated; it reveals that God was manifested in the flesh (1 Tim. 3:15-16):

1. God was manifested in the flesh not only as
the Son but as the entire God—the Father, the
Son, and the Spirit.

2. The entire God and not only God the Son was
incarnated; hence, Christ in His incarnation
was the entire God manifested in the flesh:

a. In His ministry in the stage of incarnation, Christ brought the infinite God into
the finite man; in Christ the infinite God
and the finite man became one (John 8:58;
7:6; 12:24).

b. Through incarnation the divine incorporation—God in His Divine Trinity coinhering
mutually and working together as one—
was brought into humanity; Christ is therefore the incorporation of the Triune God
with the tripartite man (14:10-11).

B. The Word, who is God, became flesh (1:1, 14):

1. The God who the Word is, is not a partial
God but the entire God—God the Son, God
the Father, and God the Spirit.

   2. The Word is God's definition, explanation, and expression; hence, the Word who became flesh—God manifested in the flesh—is God's definition, explanation, and expression in the flesh (v. 18).

 C. In Christ dwells all the fullness of the Godhead bodily (Col. 2:9):

   1. *All the fullness of the Godhead* refers to the entire Godhead, to the complete God.

   2. Since the Godhead comprises the Father, the Son, and the Spirit, the fullness of the Godhead must be the fullness of the Father, the Son, and the Spirit.

   3. That all the fullness of the Godhead dwells in Christ bodily means that the Triune God is embodied in Him (John 14:10).

   4. As the embodiment of the fullness of the Godhead, Christ is not only the Son of God but also the entire God.

*Day 3*  III. **First Timothy 3:15-16 indicates that not only**
  *&*      **Christ Himself as the Head is the manifesta-**
*Day 4*   **tion of God in the flesh but also that the church**
          **as the Body of Christ and the house of God is**
          **the manifestation of God in the flesh—the mys-**
          **tery of godliness:**

 A. *Godliness* in verse 16 refers not only to piety but also to the living of God in the church, that is, to God as life lived out in the church to be expressed:

   1. Both Christ and the church are the mystery of godliness, expressing God in the flesh.

   2. The church life is the expression of God; therefore, the mystery of godliness is the living of a proper church (1 Cor. 14:24-25).

 B. God is manifested in the church—the house of God and the Body of Christ—as His enlarged corporate expression in the flesh (Eph. 2:19; 1:22-23):

   1. The manifestation of God in the flesh began with Christ when He was on earth (John 14:9).

       2. The manifestation of God in the flesh continues with the church, which is the increase, enlargement, and multiplication of the manifestation of God in the flesh (1 Tim. 3:15-16).

  C. When a church is taken care of according to what is written in 1 Timothy 1—3, the church will function as the house of the living God for His move on earth and as the pillar and base of the truth, bearing the reality of Christ and His Body (3:15; Eph. 5:32):

       1. Such a church becomes the continuation of Christ's manifestation of God in the flesh— Christ lived out of the church as the manifestation of God.

*Day 5*        2. This is God manifested in the flesh in a wider way according to the New Testament principle of incarnation (1 Cor. 7:40; Gal. 2:20):

          a. The principle of incarnation is that God enters into man and mingles Himself with man to make man one with Himself (John 15:4-5).

          b. The principle of incarnation means that divinity is brought into humanity and works within humanity (1 Cor. 6:17; 7:40; 1 Tim. 4:1).

  D. The great mystery of godliness is that God has become man so that man may become God in life and nature but not in the Godhead to produce a corporate God-man for the manifestation of God in the flesh (Rom. 8:3; 1:3-4; Eph. 4:24).

*Day 6*  **IV. Ultimately, God will be manifested in the New Jerusalem as the consummated corporate expression of the processed and consummated Triune God in the new heaven and new earth (Rev. 21:1-2, 10-11):**

  A. The church as the manifestation of God in the flesh is the house of God, but the New

Jerusalem will be the city of God, signifying that the New Jerusalem, as the manifestation of God in the new creation, will be the enlargement and consummation of the church to express God in eternity (vv. 10-11).

B. An outstanding feature of the New Jerusalem is that it has the glory of God; the entire city bears the glory of God, which is God Himself shining out through the city (vv. 11, 23).

C. The Triune God—the Father as the source of the divine riches, the Son as the embodiment of the divine riches, and the Spirit as the realization of the divine riches—is the triune expression of the New Jerusalem for His glorious and utmost expression in His consummated manifestation for eternity (vv. 18-21; 22:1-2).

### *Morning Nourishment*

Eph. **Predestinating us unto sonship through Jesus**
1:5 **Christ to Himself, according to the good pleasure**
**of His will.**
   9 **Making known to us the mystery of His will ac-**
**cording to His good pleasure, which He purposed**
**in Himself.**
Col. **For in Him dwells all the fullness of the Godhead**
2:9 **bodily.**

God's good pleasure, God's heart's desire, is to have many
sons for the expression of His Son so that He may be expressed
in the Son through the Spirit. For this purpose, God has manifested Himself, first in Christ as an individual expression in
the flesh and then in the church, the Body of Christ, as the enlarged corporate expression in the flesh. Ultimately, God will
be manifested in the New Jerusalem as the consummated corporate expression in the new heaven and new earth. In this
message we shall consider God's manifestation in these three
stages. (*The Conclusion of the New Testament,* p. 127)

### *Today's Reading*

In the incarnation Christ is God manifested in the flesh
(1 Tim. 3:16). He was manifested in the flesh not only as the Son
but as the entire God, the Father, the Son, and the Spirit. As the
Word, who is the very God, Christ became flesh (John 1:14).
Therefore, He is God—the Triune God—manifested in the flesh.

It is important for us to realize that it was the entire God
and not only the Son of God who was incarnated. John 1:14
says that the Word, which is God, became flesh. This God, who
the Word is, is not a partial God; rather, He is the entire God—
God the Son, God the Father, and God the Spirit. The New Testament does not say that the Word, who became flesh, was God
the Son. Instead, the New Testament indicates that in the beginning was the Word, and this Word is the entire Triune God,
the Father, the Son, and the Spirit. Hence, Christ in incarnation is the entire God manifested in the flesh.

God's manifestation was first in Christ as an individual expression in the flesh. Concerning this, Colossians 2:9 says, "In Him dwells all the fullness of the Godhead bodily." In this verse "fullness" does not refer to the riches of God; instead, it refers to the expression of the riches of God. What dwells in Christ is the expression of the riches of what God is. We need to see that the fullness of the Godhead is the expression of the Godhead and that this expression is in Christ individually.

Christ is the embodiment of the fullness of the Godhead. This means that the fullness of the Triune God dwells in Christ in a bodily form. The fact that the fullness of the Godhead dwells in Christ bodily means that it dwells in Him in a way that is both real and practical. This implies the physical body which Christ put on in His humanity. It indicates that all the fullness of the Godhead dwells in Christ as the One who has a human body. Before His incarnation, the fullness of the Godhead dwelt in Him as the eternal Word, but it did not dwell in Him bodily. After He became incarnate, the fullness of the Godhead began to dwell in Him in a bodily way. Thus, He is the manifestation of God, the individual expression of God, in the flesh.

The expression "the fullness of the Godhead" refers to the entire Godhead, to the complete God, including the Father, the Son, and the Spirit. Because the Godhead comprises the Father, the Son, and the Spirit, it would not be correct to say that the fullness of the Godhead includes only God the Son and not also God the Father and God the Spirit. Since the Godhead comprises the Father, the Son, and the Spirit, the fullness of the Godhead must be the fullness of the Father, the Son, and the Spirit. As the embodiment of the fullness of the Godhead, Christ is not only the Son of God but the entire God. (*The Conclusion of the New Testament,* pp. 281, 127-128)

*Further Reading: The Conclusion of the New Testament,* msgs. 13, 16, 26

**Enlightenment and inspiration:** _____
_____
_____
_____

## *Morning Nourishment*

John In the beginning was the Word, and the Word was
1:1 with God, and the Word was God.
14 And the Word became flesh and tabernacled among
us (and we beheld His glory, glory as of the only Begotten from the Father), full of grace and reality.
14:10 Do you not believe that I am in the Father and the
Father is in Me?...

John 1:1 and 14...reveal that God was manifested in Christ as
an individual expression in the flesh. Verse 1 says, "In the beginning was the Word, and the Word was with God, and the Word
was God." In verse 14, this Word, which is God, became flesh. This
refers to the incarnated Christ. In the beginning He was not only
with God but He is the very God. The incarnated Christ is God
manifested in the flesh (1 Tim. 3:16).

John 1 further says, "No one has ever seen God; the only begotten Son, who is in the bosom of the Father, He has declared Him"
(v. 18). This tells us that Christ, being the only begotten Son of
God, is the expression of God. No one has ever seen God, yet He
declares God. The Father is the invisible God, the hidden God;
Christ is the manifested God.

When we say that Christ is the Word, we are saying that He is
the expression of God. I may have a great deal of feeling within
me, but if I have no words, my feelings cannot be expressed. But
when my feelings are expressed in words, then you are able to understand them. Christ is the Word of God. Although no one knows
God, Christ as the Word speaks for God, defines God, and even declares God. (*The Conclusion of the New Testament*, pp. 128-129)

### *Today's Reading*

Because God is abstract, mysterious, and invisible, there is the
need for God to be the Word in order to explain Himself, define
Himself, and reveal Himself. The Word in John 1:1 refers to the defined God, the explained and expressed God, the God revealed and
made known to human beings. This Word is our Lord Jesus Christ,
the living Word of God. The Word is the embodiment of the Triune

God. Although the Triune God is mysterious, He is nonetheless embodied in the Word. The Word is the definition, explanation, and expression of the mysterious and invisible God. The Triune God embodied in the Word is explained, defined, and expressed.

In John 1:14, the Word, the embodiment of the Triune God, became flesh. In the incarnated Christ God is expressed in a man in the flesh. This is according to God's plan. God's plan is to manifest Himself in man and through man in the flesh.

John 1:14 continues to say that the Word, after becoming flesh "tabernacled among us (and we beheld His glory, glory as of the only Begotten from the Father), full of grace and reality." This indicates that the Word was incarnated to declare God. As the manifestation of God, Christ declared God in a way that was full of grace and reality. He declared God by presenting Himself as grace and reality. God, the very God of enjoyment, becomes grace and reality to us in Christ for our enjoyment. Through enjoying Him we gain Him as grace and reality. He declares God to man in the way of enjoyment.

When we enjoy God in Christ as grace and realize Him in Christ as reality, we find the unsearchable riches of Christ. John 1:16 says, "Of His fullness we have all received, and grace upon grace." In the incarnated Christ dwells all the fullness, the expression of the riches of God (Col. 2:9). Through His incarnation in Christ, we can receive the riches of grace and reality out of His divine fullness.

Christ as the Father's only begotten Son declared God by the Word, life, light, grace, and reality (John 1:1, 4, 9, 14). The Word is God expressed, life is God imparted, light is God shining, grace is God enjoyed, and reality is God realized. It is by these things that God is declared in the Son as His individual expression. Christ explained, defined, declared, and expressed God, by being the Word incarnated to be life and light to man with grace and reality for man's enjoyment. It is in this way, God was declared to man in the Son. (*The Conclusion of the New Testament*, pp. 129-130)

*Further Reading: The Conclusion of the New Testament*, msg. 13

### *Enlightenment and inspiration:* _____

_____

_____

_____

## Morning Nourishment

1 Tim.  But if I delay, *I write* that you may know how one
3:15-16  ought to conduct himself in the house of God, which
is the church of the living God, the pillar and base of
the truth. And confessedly, great is the mystery of
godliness: He who was manifested in the flesh, justified in the Spirit, seen by angels, preached among the
nations, believed on in the world, taken up in glory.

1 Cor.  But if all prophesy and some unbeliever or unlearned
14:24-25  person enters, he is convicted by all, he is examined
by all; the secrets of his heart become manifest; and so
falling on *his* face, he will worship God, declaring that
indeed God is among you.

We have pointed out that the fullness of God is the expression
of God. According to John 1:16, the fullness of God came with
Christ, who is the embodiment of God's fullness. With Christ,
the expression of God was an individual matter. This expression
needs to be enlarged from an individual to a corporate expression. The church is to be the enlarged corporate expression of
God in the flesh. This means that the church should be the fullness, the expression of God, in a corporate way. In the church
God is expressed not through an individual but corporately
through the Body of Christ. Because the fullness of God is embodied in the church, the church is the corporate expression of
the Triune God. (*The Conclusion of the New Testament*, p. 130)

## Today's Reading

First Timothy 3:15 and 16 indicate that God is manifested in
the church—the Body of Christ—as the enlarged corporate expression in the flesh: "The house of God, which is the church of
the living God, the pillar and base of the truth. And confessedly,
great is the mystery of godliness, He who was manifested in the
flesh, justified in the Spirit, seen by angels, preached among the
nations, believed on in the world, taken up in glory." In Greek the
antecedent of "who" is omitted but easily recognized, that is,
Christ who was God manifested in the flesh as the mystery of

godliness. The transition from "the mystery…" to "who" implies that Christ as the manifestation of God in the flesh is the mystery of godliness (Col. 1:27; Gal. 2:20). This mystery of godliness is the living of a proper church, and such a living is also the manifestation of God in the flesh.

These verses imply that not only Christ Himself as the Head but also the church as the Body is the manifestation of God in the flesh. When a church grows in Christ with the growth of God (Col. 2:19), it will function as the house and household of the living God for His move on the earth and as the supporting pillar and holding base of the truth, bearing the divine reality of Christ and His Body as a testimony to the world. Then the church becomes the continuation of Christ's manifestation of God in the flesh. This is the great mystery of godliness—Christ lived out of the church as the manifestation of God in the flesh.

Such a church is the continuation, the enlargement and expansion of God manifested in the flesh. This manifestation of God is the church as the house of God and the pillar and base of the truth. The church is, then, the increase, the enlargement, of the manifestation of God in the flesh. This is God manifested in the flesh in a wider way. This is according to the New Testament principle of incarnation, which is God manifested in the flesh.

First Timothy 3:16 begins with the words, "And confessedly, great is the mystery of godliness." The conjunction "and" here indicates that the speaking about the church in verse 15 is not finished yet, and that the church is something even more than the house of the living God and the pillar and base of the truth. The church is also the mystery of godliness. According to the context, godliness refers to the living of God in the church, that is, God as life lived out in the church to be expressed. The church life is the expression of God. Both Christ and the church, the Head and the Body, are the mystery of godliness, expressing God in the flesh. (*The Conclusion of the New Testament*, pp. 130-132)

*Further Reading: The Conclusion of the New Testament*, msg. 13

### *Enlightenment and inspiration:* _____

_____

_____

_____

## Morning Nourishment

1 Tim. ...In the house of God, which is the church of the living
3:15-16 God, the pillar and base of the truth. And confessedly,
great is the mystery of godliness: He who was manifested in the flesh, justified in the Spirit, seen by angels, preached among the nations, believed on in the
world, taken up in glory.

Gal. I am crucified with Christ; and *it is* no longer I *who*
2:20 live, but *it is* Christ *who* lives in me; and the *life* which I
now live in the flesh I live in faith, the *faith* of the Son
of God, who loved me and gave Himself up for me.

The church as the house of the living God and as the pillar and
base of the truth is not so mysterious. But the church as the manifestation of God in the flesh certainly is a mystery. A mystery
always goes beyond our understanding. It refers to something
which cannot be explained. If we are able to explain a certain
matter, it is not a mystery.

The church is not only the house of the living God and the pillar and base of the truth, but also the mystery of godliness. Godliness refers to God expressed. What are we doing in the church
life? We are expressing God. Human beings may not realize this
adequately, but the angels recognize it and appreciate it. On the
one hand, the good angels rejoice when they behold the expression of God in the church. On the other hand, the evil angels and
the demons tremble in fear. They realize that eventually those in
the church life will condemn them to the lake of fire. (*Life-study of
1 Timothy*, p. 57)

## Today's Reading

The first part of 1 Timothy 3:16 speaks of a matter—the mystery of godliness. Hence, we would expect Paul to use the relative
pronoun "which" to refer to the mystery of godliness as a matter.
However, the fact that he uses the relative pronoun "who" implies
that the mystery of godliness is a person and not merely a matter.
As we shall see, this person is Christ as the Head with His Body.

Through incarnation and human living (John 1:1, 14), God was manifested in the flesh. "In the flesh" means in the likeness, in the fashion, of man (Rom. 8:3; Phil. 2:7-8). In the form of man Christ appeared to people (2 Cor. 5:16), yet He was God manifested in a man. Christ was also "justified in the Spirit." The Greek word also means vindicated. The incarnated Christ in His human living was not only vindicated as the Son of God by the Spirit (Matt. 3:16-17; Rom. 1:3-4), but was also justified, proved, and approved as right and righteous by the Spirit (Matt. 3:15-16; 4:1).

Paul also says "seen by angels." Angels saw the incarnation, human living, and ascension of Christ (Luke 2:9-14; Matt. 4:11; Acts 1:10-11; Rev. 5:6, 11-12). Christ was also preached among the nations. Christ as God's manifestation in the flesh has been preached as the gospel among the nations, including the nation of Israel, from the day of Pentecost (Rom. 16:26; Eph. 3:8). Further-more, Christ has been "believed on in the world." Christ as the embodiment of God in the flesh has been believed on, received as Savior and life, by people in the world (Acts 13:48).

Paul concludes verse 16 with the phrase "taken up in glory." This refers to Christ's ascension into glory (Mark 16:19; Acts 1:9-11; 2:33; Phil. 2:9). According to the sequence of historical events, Christ's ascension preceded His being preached among the nations. However, it is listed here as the last event of Christ being the manifestation of God in the flesh. This seems to indicate the church taken up in glory. Hence, it implies that not only Christ Himself as the Head, but also the church as the Body, is the manifestation of God in the flesh.

In 1 Timothy 3:16 there is a definite indication that this verse refers not only to the Head as the manifestation of God in the flesh, but also to the Body as the continuation of this manifesta-tion....The Head, Christ, has been taken up in glory, and the Body, the church, will also be taken up in glory. Both the Head and the Body are the mystery of godliness. This is the manifestation of God in the flesh. (*Life-study of 1 Timothy,* pp. 58-60)

*Further Reading: Life-study of 1 Timothy,* msg. 6

***Enlightenment and inspiration:*** _____

_____
_____
_____

*Morning Nourishment*

John 15:5   I am the vine; you are the branches. He who
             abides in Me and I in him, he bears much
             fruit; for apart from Me you can do nothing.
Eph. 4:24   And put on the new man, which was created
             according to God in righteousness and holi-
             ness of the reality.
1 Cor. 6:17   But he who is joined to the Lord is one spirit.

To be regenerated is to be resurrected with the divine life.
Therefore, today we should live a life conformed to the death of
Christ (Phil. 3:10) that the divine life may have an opportunity
to live with our resurrected humanity....This is for the manifestation of God in the flesh as the new man (1 Tim. 3:16; Eph.
2:15). First Timothy 3:16 says, "And confessedly, great is the
mystery of godliness: He who was manifested in the flesh."...
Godliness here refers not only to piety but also to the living
of God in the church, that is, to God as life lived out in the
church. Godliness means that God becomes man and man
becomes God. This is a great mystery in the universe. God
has become man so that man may become God to produce a corporate God-man for the manifestation of God in the flesh as the
new man. (*The God-men,* pp. 14-15)

## *Today's Reading*

In the church God dwells, because the church is the house of
God. God lives, God moves, and God works out His life *in the
church;* and the testimony and the reality stand *upon the
church.* We must consider these two aspects: *inwardly,* God's
dwelling in the church; and *outwardly,* the church bearing the
testimony and the reality. These two aspects show the real
mingling of God with man. Within the church—this group of
redeemed, regenerated, and transformed people—God dwells;
and upon this group of people, there is the reality of the universe. All the reality of the universe is centered in this group. If
anyone wants to know what life is, he must come to the church
and see. If some would like to know what love is, they too must

come and see. If the reality of humility and kindness is to be known, the church is the place to see it. Upon this group of people is seen the reality of the all-inclusive Christ. The testimony of the church is not in doctrine but in bearing Christ as the reality....The church must be the pillar and base, bearing Christ as the only reality of everything.

This is the right meaning of "the house of God" and "the pillar and base of the truth." This church is the *continuation* and the *multiplication* of God "manifest in the flesh." This is the reason why the apostle Paul put these two verses together. The manifestation of God in the flesh has very much to do with the church being the house of God and the pillar and base of truth. When we are the living Body of Christ in a certain place, we are really the house of God and the pillar and base of reality. We are then the *increase,* the *enlargement,* of the manifestation of God in the flesh. God manifests Himself again in the flesh, but in a *wider* way. The principle of the New Testament is the principle of the incarnation, which simply is: God Himself manifest in the flesh. In other words, God is mingled with human beings— not in an outward way, but in an inward way. The church is the manifestation of God, not the manifestation of doctrines or gifts. The church must have God in Christ through the Spirit manifested, not the doctrines or gifts demonstrated.

God's intention is to impart Christ into us and make Christ everything within us....Inner revelation is needed to see the goal of the living Christ dwelling within us. Then, wherever we are meeting together, we are the living house of the living God. The living God dwells, lives, and works in us; and we bear the testimony of Jesus, who is the reality of this whole universe. Then we will have a real manifestation of the living God in the flesh. This is the way of God's recovery today. Let us look to the Lord for the inner grace that we may have the reality of the church. (*The Economy of God,* pp. 198-199, 204)

*Further Reading: The God-men,* ch. 1; *The Economy of God,* ch. 23

*Enlightenment and inspiration:* _____

_____

_____

## *Morning Nourishment*

Rev.  And he carried me away in spirit onto a great and
21:10-11  high mountain and showed me the holy city, Jerusalem, coming down out of heaven from God, having
the glory of God. Her light was like a most precious
stone, like a jasper stone, as clear as crystal.
18  And the building work of its wall was jasper; and the
city was pure gold, like clear glass.
23  And the city has no need of the sun or of the moon
that they should shine in it, for the glory of God illumined it, and its lamp is the Lamb.

The final stage of God's manifestation will be in the New Jerusalem as the consummated corporate expression in the new creation
[Rev. 21:1-3]....In eternity past God purposed to have a corporate
expression so that He might be fully expressed and glorified (Eph.
3:9-11; 1:9-11). For this, He created the heavens, the earth, and man-
kind. Eventually, the old heaven and the old earth will pass away
through fire and be renewed into the new heaven and new earth
(2 Pet. 3:10-13) into which the New Jerusalem will come for God's
eternal expression. (*The Conclusion of the New Testament*, p. 132)

## *Today's Reading*

Today the church, as the manifestation of God in the flesh, is the
house of God, whereas in the new heaven and new earth the New
Jerusalem, as the manifestation of God in the new creation, will be
the city of God. The city is much bigger than the house, signifying
that the New Jerusalem, as the manifestation of God in His new
creation, will be the enlargement and consummation of the church
to express God in eternity.

At the beginning of the Scripture in God's old creation there was
a garden, the garden of Eden (Gen. 2:8). At the end of the Scripture
in God's new creation there will be a city, the city of the New Jerusalem. The garden and the city at the two ends of the Scripture
reflect each other, with the tree of life which is in both of them as
the link (Gen. 2:9; Rev. 22:2). The garden was the issue of God's creation; whereas the city will be the consummation of God's building,

a building which God has been carrying out through all the dispensations—the dispensation of the patriarchs, the dispensation of the law, the dispensation of grace, and the dispensation of the kingdom—of the old creation. Out of His old creation through all the dispensations, God has been doing His building work in the way of regeneration and resurrection. The ultimate result and the ultimate consummation of this building work will be the New Jerusalem in the new heaven and new earth as God's manifestation in His new creation for eternity. It is not a creation by God's divine power in the way to call things not being as being; but it is a building by God's divine life in the way to regenerate the things which exist with the resurrection life that they may be one with God in His divine life and nature for His expression.

Revelation 21:11 and 23 tell us that the New Jerusalem has the glory of God and her light was like a most precious stone, as jasper stone, clear as crystal. It has no need of the sun or of the moon that they should shine in it, for the glory of God illumines it, and its lamp is the Lamb. The glory of God, which is God expressed, illumines the New Jerusalem. Hence, the glory of God, with God as its substance, essence, and elements, is the light of the New Jerusalem, which shines in the Lamb as its lamp. The expressed glory of God, or the God of glory expressed, is the light shining in Christ as the lamp through the jasper wall of the New Jerusalem like the most precious jasper...for God's expression in His final and consummated manifestation.

The New Jerusalem is really a marvelous mingling of the processed Triune God with His chosen, redeemed, regenerated, sanctified, transformed, conformed, built, and glorified tripartite people for His glorious and utmost expression in His consummated manifestation for eternity, in the new creation of resurrection, no longer in the natural flesh, as His individual manifestation in Christ and His corporate manifestation were in the past. (*The Conclusion of the New Testament,* pp. 133-134, 137-140)

*Further Reading: The Conclusion of the New Testament,* msgs. 13, 219

### *Enlightenment and inspiration:* _____

_____

_____
_____

*Hymns,* #819

1   As the body is the fulness
      To express our life,
    So to Christ the church, His Body,
      Doth express His life.

2   E'en as Eve is part of Adam
      Taken out of him,
    So the church is Christ's own increase
      With Himself within.

3   As from out the buried kernel
      Many grains are formed,
    As the grains together blended
      To a loaf are formed;

4   So the church, of many Christians,
      Christ doth multiply,
    Him expressing as one Body,
      God to glorify.

5   As the branches of the grapevine
      Are its outward spread,
    With it one, abiding, bearing
      Clusters in its stead;

6   So the church's many members
      Christ's enlargement are,
    One with Him in life and living,
      Spreading Him afar.

7   Fulness, increase, duplication,
      His expression full,
    Growth and spread, continuation,
      Surplus plentiful,

8   Is the church to Christ, and thereby
      God in Christ may be
    Glorified thru His redeemed ones
      To eternity.

9   Thus the church and Christ together,
      God's great mystery,
    Is the mingling of the Godhead
      With humanity.

*Composition for prophecy with main point and sub-points:* _____

_____

_____

_____

_____

_____

_____

_____

_____

_____

_____

_____

_____

_____

_____

_____

_____

_____

_____

_____

_____

_____

_____

_____

_____

_____

_____

_____

_____

_____

_____

_____

_____

_____

_____

## *The Exercise of Our Spirit unto Godliness*

Scripture Reading: 1 Tim. 4:7-8; 2 Tim. 1:6-7; 4:22

*Day 1*

I. **In the "blueprint" of God's original intention, man is the center of the entire universe, and the center of man is his spirit (Zech. 12:1; Gen. 2:7):**

A. The heavens are for the earth, the earth is for man, and man was created by God with a spirit that he may contact God, receive God, contain God, worship God, live God, fulfill God's purpose for God, express God, and be one with God (Prov. 20:27; John 4:24; 1 Cor. 6:17).

B. Without God being the Spirit and without us having a spirit to contact God, to be one with God, the whole universe is empty and we are nothing (Eccl. 1:2; 3:11; Job 32:8; 12:10; 2 Cor. 4:13, 16-18).

C. Due to the fall, men have not only overlooked and neglected the human spirit but also have even refused to admit that man has a spirit (cf. 1 Thes. 5:23; Heb. 4:12; Jude 19).

D. Man as a vessel, through the exercise of his spirit, was to receive God in Christ as the tree of life so that life as a river would flow in and out of his innermost being for his transformation into precious materials for God's building, God's eternal expression (Gen. 1:26; 2:7-12, 22; 1 Tim. 4:7-8):

1. The breath of God has become our human spirit, and our spirit is God's lamp to contain God as the oil and to give us light (Gen. 2:7; Prov. 20:27).

2. Man's spirit became a broken lamp through his fall, but through God's recovery in His salvation, man's spirit is regenerated, rebuilt, and reinforced with the vivifying, sevenfold intensified Spirit (Gen. 2:7; Prov. 20:27; John 3:6; Rev. 4:5; 1 Cor. 15:45b).

3. The central government and most prominent

part of man's being should be his spirit; a man who is ruled and controlled by his spirit is a spiritual man (2:14-15; 3:1; 14:32; Eph. 3:16; 1 Pet. 3:4; Dan. 6:3, 10).

E. The building of God into man is typified by both the tabernacle and the breastplate, and the key to God's building is our mingled spirit:

1. The uniting bars of the boards of the tabernacle, made of acacia wood overlaid with gold, signify the mingled spirit, the divine Spirit mingled with the human spirit to become the uniting bond of peace (Exo. 26:26-30; Rom. 8:16; Eph. 4:3-4).

2. In the New Testament the reality of the Urim and the Thummim put into the breastplate is the mingled spirit—the unveiling Spirit of God, the Holy Spirit, indwelling our receiving spirit, our regenerated human spirit (Exo. 28:30; Rom. 8:4, 14; 1 Cor. 2:9-12).

F. The divine Spirit dwelling in our human spirit and the two mingled together as one spirit, the mingled spirit, is the strategic and central point of God's economy (John 3:6; Rom. 8:16; 2 Tim. 4:22; 1 Cor. 6:17; 1 Tim. 1:4; 2 Cor. 4:13):

1. The great way to fulfill God's economy is for us to live and do everything according to the Spirit by exercising our spirit (Job 10:13; Eph. 3:9; Rom. 8:4; Gal. 5:25).

2. Whenever we turn to our spirit and exercise our spirit, we touch the Body, because the Body is in our spirit (Eph. 1:17; 2:22; 3:5, 16; 4:23; 5:18; 6:18).

3. When we are in our spirit, we overcome the world, we cannot sin, the evil one cannot touch us, and we are guarded from idols (1 John 5:4, 18-19, 21).

*Day 2*  II. **The subject of 2 Timothy is the inoculation against the decline of the church, and the key to receiving and dispensing this inoculation** is the exercise of our spirit (1:6-7; 1 Tim. 4:7-8; Acts 6:10; 1 Cor. 14:32):

A. Godliness, a living that is the expression of God, is the issue of the divine dispensing for the divine economy, and this dispensing depends on the exercise of our spirit to live Christ in our daily life for the corporate manifestation of God in the church life (1 Tim. 1:3-4; 3:15-16; 4:7-8; 2 Tim. 1:6-7).

B. The word *exercise* implies forcing; if we Christians want to be strong and want to grow in the Lord, we must force ourselves to use our spirit until we build up a strong habit of exercising our spirit (1 Tim. 4:7).

*Day 3*

C. To exercise our spirit is to fan our spirit into flame (2 Tim. 1:6-7):

1. Fire is in our regenerated spirit, which is indwelt by the Holy Spirit; actually, our spirit is the fire (cf. Luke 12:49-50; Rom. 12:11).

2. We saved ones have the capital to live the Christian life and the church life; this capital is our God-given spirit.

D. To exercise our spirit we must deal with the parts of our heart surrounding our spirit—our mind, emotion, will, and conscience (1 Pet. 3:4; Psa. 51:10):

1. A spirit of power is a spirit with a subdued and resurrected will, a spirit of love is a spirit with an emotion filled with God as love, and a spirit of sobermindedness is a spirit with a renewed mind (2 Tim. 1:7).

2. To exercise our spirit is to exercise ourselves to have a good conscience without offense toward God and men and to have a pure conscience, which means to have a pure heart of seeking only God and His will (1 Tim. 1:19; 3:9; 2 Tim. 1:3; Acts 23:1; 24:16; Matt. 5:8; Psa. 73:25-26).

*Day 4*

E. To exercise our spirit by rejoicing always, praying unceasingly, and giving thanks in everything to

enjoy the indwelling Spirit is the secret of doing
all things in Christ (2 Cor. 12:2a; Phil. 4:11-13;
Psa. 91:1; 1 Thes. 5:16-18).

F. To exercise our spirit is to pray, to approach God in
a personal and confiding manner, for the interests
of God—Christ, the kingdom of God, and the
house of God—as the goal in God's eternal economy (2 Tim. 1:6-8; 1 Tim. 1:3-4; 2:1-3, 8; 1 Kings
8:48; Jude 19-21).

*Day 5*

G. To exercise our spirit is to set our mind on the
spirit (Rom. 8:6; Mal. 2:15-16):

1. When we set our mind on the spirit, we have
the inner sense of life and peace, the sense of
strength, satisfaction, rest, release, liveli-
ness, watering, brightness, and comfort.

2. When we set our mind on the flesh, we have
the inner sense of death, the sense of weakness, emptiness, uneasiness, restlessness,
depression, dryness, darkness, and pain.

3. Our Christian life is not according to the
standard of right and wrong but according to
the spirit, and we know the spirit by the
inner sense of life and peace (Rom. 8:6; 2 Cor.
2:13-14).

*Day 6*

H. To exercise our spirit is to discern our spirit from
our soul (Heb. 4:12):

1. We should always be on the alert to discern
and deny anything that is not of the spirit
but of the soul, the self (Matt. 16:25; cf. Luke
9:25).

2. Whatever we are, whatever we have, and
whatever we do must be in spirit; everything
that God is to us is in our spirit (Rom. 2:28-29;
1:9; 8:4; 12:11).

I. To exercise our spirit is to live the normal church
life and overcome the church's degradation by
pursuing Christ with those who call on the Lord
out of a pure heart (2 Tim. 2:22).

## *Morning Nourishment*

Zech. ...*Thus* declares Jehovah, who stretches forth the
12:1  heavens and lays the foundations of the earth and
      forms the spirit of man within him.
Gen.  Jehovah God formed man from the dust of the
2:7   ground and breathed into his nostrils the breath of
      life, and man became a living soul.
John  God is Spirit, and those who worship Him must
4:24  worship in spirit and truthfulness.
1 Cor. But he who is joined to the Lord is one spirit.
6:17

Genesis tells us clearly that in God's creation, He did something particular to produce our spirit (2:7). God created the universe by speaking. God spoke and it was (Psa. 33:9). But when
God came to the creation of man, He breathed His breath of life
into man. Our breath is not ourselves, but nothing is as close to us
as our breath. In like manner, God's breath of life is not God Himself, not the divine Spirit, and not the divine life, but it is very close
to God, close to the divine Spirit, and close to the divine life.

If we did not have a spirit, we would be like the beasts. We
would become meaningless. Also, if there were no God in the
universe, the whole universe would become empty. So the key to
our meaning and the meaning of the universe is in God's existence and also in our having a spirit. God is Spirit and we must
contact Him, worship Him, in our spirit (John 4:24). These two
spirits should contact each other and should become one (1 Cor.
6:17). Then the whole universe becomes meaningful. Then our
life has its meaning. Without God being the Spirit and without
us having a spirit to contact God, to be one with God, the whole
universe is empty and we are nothing. By this we can see the importance of our spirit. (*The Spirit with Our Spirit*, p. 78)

## *Today's Reading*

Regrettably, due to the fall, men have not only overlooked and
neglected the human spirit, but also have even refused to admit
that man has a spirit. Some men who live a higher life take care of
their conscience, but they are in the minority. Most people take

care of the law, not their conscience. Today's society needs the law so much because most people neglect one part of their spirit— their conscience. The conscience functions to judge us and condemn us when we do something wrong....Some who are governed merely by the law like to find loopholes in the law so that they can carry out things that are unrighteous and unjust. Those who live by the conscience, however, live in a higher way. Our inward conscience controls us much more than the outward law does.

As Christians, our spirit has been regenerated. To be regenerated is to be reinforced. Something stronger and richer has been added into our being. This is God's life, which has been added into our spirit. This addition is a real gift. Hebrews 6:4 says that we believers have tasted of the heavenly gift. When we believe in the Lord Jesus, God firstly gives us the divine life. Secondly, God gives us the Holy Spirit. Also, He gives us many heavenly things, such as His forgiveness, righteousness, peace, and joy. God has given us justification, reconciliation, and His full salvation....All these heavenly things are included in God's life and God's Spirit, which have been added into our spirit. We have a regenerated and reinforced spirit, a very strong spirit, with a companion. This companion is the Triune God. The Triune God becomes our companion in our spirit. What an enriched spirit we have!

Now that we have seen the importance of our spirit, we want to see the exercise of our spirit. We must build up a habit of exercising our spirit. When I rise up in the morning, the first thing I spontaneously say is "O Lord." To call on the Lord by saying, "O Lord" is a habit of exercising our spirit. To say "O Lord" as soon as you rise up in the morning makes a big difference. If you rise up in the morning without saying anything, you may pray in a routine way without really touching the Lord. This is because there is no exercise of your spirit. We have to build up a habit of saying, "O Lord." When we say, "O Lord," we touch the Lord. This is the habit of exercising our spirit. (*The Spirit with Our Spirit,* pp. 78-79)

*Further Reading: The Spirit with Our Spirit,* ch. 8

***Enlightenment and inspiration:*** _____

_____

_____

## Morning Nourishment

1 Tim.   But the profane and old-womanish myths refuse, and
4:7-8   exercise yourself unto godliness. For bodily exercise
         is profitable for a little, but godliness is profitable for
         all things, having promise of the present life and of
         that which is to come.
2 Tim.   For which cause I remind you to fan into flame the gift
1:6-7    of God, which is in you through the laying on of my
         hands. For God has not given us a spirit of cowardice,
         but of power and of love and of sobermindedness.

At times we may be in a hard situation. We may be sick or
we may have lost our job. At that time, we should exercise our
spirit. We should force ourselves to say, "O Lord Jesus!" The
word *exercise* implies forcing. To exercise is always a forced
matter. When the Olympic athletes are exercising to practice
or compete, they must have a strong will. They force themselves to exercise. If we Christians want to be strong and want
to grow in the Lord, we must force ourselves to use our spirit.

Whenever you are in a hard situation, you have to force
yourself to exercise your spirit. To force yourself to exercise, or
to use, your spirit makes you a different person.

In 1 Timothy 4:7 Paul said, "Exercise yourself unto godliness." Then in verse 8 he spoke of bodily exercise. In these two
verses Paul speaks of two kinds of exercise. The exercise be-
sides that of the body, which is the exercise unto godliness,
must be the exercise of the spirit. To exercise ourselves unto
godliness is to exercise our spirit to live Christ in our daily life.
(*The Spirit with Our Spirit,* pp. 79-80)

## Today's Reading

Second Timothy 1:6-7 indicates that we need to fan our
spirit into flame....Some might think that these verses do not
say that we should fan our spirit, but that we should fan our
gift. But if you get into these verses, you will see that the fanning of our gift into flame is the fanning of our spirit into
flame. Paul tells us in verse 6 to "fan into flame the gift of

God." Then in verse 7 he says, "For God has not given us a spirit..." Our God-given spirit is what we must fan into flame. We have to fan our spirit.

We have to know the background of 2 Timothy to appreciate Paul's word here. Paul wrote this book during a difficult time for his spiritual son Timothy. Paul was in prison in Rome. Furthermore, all those in Asia had forsaken Paul's ministry (v. 15). The churches in Asia were the main churches raised up through Paul's ministry, but they forsook him. Timothy was there among them....No doubt, Timothy was discouraged. Otherwise, Paul would not have said, "For which cause I remind you...."...Paul knew Timothy was down and he sympathized with him. He reminded Timothy that there was still a small fire within him which he needed to fan into flame.

At times you may suffer to such an extent that you may begin to doubt God and doubt your salvation. But regardless of how much you doubt, one thing is within you which you cannot deny—your spirit. You are not like a beast. You have a spirit. This spirit is a trouble to Satan. Regardless of how much work Satan has done and is still doing, there is one thing within that he cannot touch—our spirit. We need to fan our spirit into flame.

If you want to fan your spirit into flame, you need to open up your mouth, open up your heart, and open up your spirit. You need to open these three layers of your being. You have to use your mouth to say, "O Lord Jesus." But then you have to go deeper by using your mouth with your heart to say, "O Lord Jesus." Then you need to go even deeper by using your mouth with your heart and with your spirit to say, "O Lord Jesus." This is to open up your spirit from deep within. Then the fire burns. If you are down, you should call, "O Lord Jesus" again and again from deep within with the exercise of your spirit. Then you will be up. (*The Spirit with Our Spirit,* pp. 80-82)

*Further Reading: The Spirit with Our Spirit,* ch. 8

***Enlightenment and inspiration:*** _____

_____

_____
_____

## *Morning Nourishment*

2 Tim.  For which cause I remind you to fan into flame the gift
1:6-7  of God, which is in you through the laying on of my
        hands. For God has not given us a spirit of cowardice,
        but of power and of love and of sobermindedness.
Rom.    Do not be slothful in zeal, *but* be burning in spirit,
12:11   serving the Lord.

Verses 6 and 7 of 2 Timothy 1 are marvelous. These verses
show us that we saved ones have the capital to live the Christian
life and the church life. This capital is the God-given spirit. This
God-given spirit, according to God's ordination, is surrounded by
the power of our will, by the love of our emotion, and by the
sobermindedness of our mind. These three helpers are surrounding our spirit, not to depress us, but rather to uplift us and help us.

We have to exercise such a God-given spirit. The capital for a
person to run in a race is his God-created legs. Without God cre-
ating two legs for you, how could you run? You have no capital to
run. In like manner, if God did not give us a spirit, we would not
have the capital to run the Christian race. But today we have a
great account, a great deposit in the bank. We have a God-given
spirit. As long as we have the God-given spirit, we have power,
love, and a sober mind with a clear sky.

To say that we have the capital means that we have the capacity. We can do things because we have the capacity of power. We
should not say that we do not love people, because we have the capacity of love. We should not say that we are in darkness, because
we have the capacity of sobermindedness with a clear sky. We
should declare, "My sky is not cloudy; my sky is clear," because
this is our capacity. (*The Spirit with Our Spirit*, pp. 82-83)

## *Today's Reading*

Quite often we are cheated and deceived by the enemy. We
say that we are weak and cloudy. But when we say we are weak,
we are weak. When we say we are cloudy, we are cloudy. On the
other hand, when we say we are strong, we are strong. When we
say we are clear, we are clear. When we say what we are, that is

what we are. Do not say you are weak. If you say you are weak, weakness is with you. But if you say you are strong, strength is with you. We can say we are strong because we have the capacity. We have the capital. God gave us, not a spirit of cowardice but a spirit of power, of love, and of sobermindedness. We should declare this and claim this. Then we will have it. This is our portion. This is our legal, God-appointed lot, which has been allotted to us by God.

I am sharing this to point out that you should not listen to what you feel or what you think. What you feel and what you think are altogether a lie, a falsehood. Christians should not believe that. We should always believe and declare and claim that we are strong. We are full of love. We can love our enemies. We are well able to love everybody. We are very clear. Our sky is crystal clear. You have to believe because you have this capital. This is your capacity. You should claim and declare, "I am strong! I am loving! I am clear!" You are blessed if you say this. This is the way to exercise your spirit. This is to fan your spirit into flame. Then you will pray. The more you pray, the more you are fanning, and the more burning there will be within you.

Whenever there is the fanning, there is always a battle with Satan. While the fanning of a fire is going on, the fire department is fighting to quench the fire. This is an illustration of Satan trying to quench the fire being fanned within us. Today there are many things that are like cold water, trying to quench our inner flame. Sometimes a telephone call comes with bad news. Then someone comes to you with more bad news. Things will happen in our environment which can quench us. At that time, we have to fight. We have to declare the facts. We have to fan our spirit into flame. Then we will be the highest persons, the super persons. (*The Spirit with Our Spirit*, pp. 83-84)

*Further Reading: The Spirit with Our Spirit*, ch. 8; *The Stream*, vol. 5, no. 1; *The Scriptural Way to Meet and to Serve for the Building Up of the Body of Christ*, ch. 15

***Enlightenment and inspiration:*** _____

_____

_____

## *Morning Nourishment*

1 Tim. **I exhort therefore, first of all, that petitions, prayers,**
2:1-3 **intercessions, thanksgivings be made on behalf of**
**all men; on behalf of kings and all who are in high**
**position, that we may lead a quiet and tranquil life**
**in all godliness and gravity. This is good and accept-**
**able in the sight of our Savior God.**
8 **I desire therefore that men pray in every place, lift-**
**ing up holy hands, without wrath and reasoning.**

In the first chapter of 1 Timothy, Paul lays a good foundation to speak of the church life in a positive way. In 2:1 he goes on....If we would have a proper church life, we must first have a prayer life. The leading ones, those who minister the Word in the church, should take the lead to have such a prayer life. A prayer ministry is the prerequisite for the administration and shepherding of a local church. Thus, Paul exhorts Timothy that petitions, prayers, intercessions, and thanksgivings be made on behalf of all men. This is the first word concerning the positive aspect of the church life Paul gives after speaking of God's economy and after charging Timothy to war the good warfare for God's economy. Timothy had to take the lead to have a prayer life.

A prerequisite for having a proper church life in the Lord's recovery today is to have a prayer life. A proper church is a praying church. A church that is without prayer is pitiful. Prayerlessness is a sin. All in the Lord's recovery must be prayerful and stand against the sin of prayerlessness. The elders in the churches must take up Paul's charge to "first of all" pray. (*Life-study of 1 Timothy*, p. 25)

## *Today's Reading*

If we would be a Timothy, we must take the lead not to argue, gossip, or criticize, but to pray. Whenever we hear some news, good or bad, concerning a particular church, we should pray. Do not discuss the situation, do not gossip about it, and do not criticize. Just pray! Likewise, if you hear something about a saint or about an elder, pray for that one. The first requirement to have a proper church life is to pray. Oh, we all need to practice this! If we exercise ourselves to have a prayer life, the church will be living and uplifted.

In 2:1 Paul mentions petitions, prayers, intercessions, and thanksgivings. Prayer is general, with the essence of worship and fellowship. Petitions are special and are for particular needs. The Greek word rendered "intercessions" means approach to God in a personal and confiding manner, that is, intervene, interfere, before God in others' affairs for their benefit. In addition, we must offer thanksgiving. Often when we hear good news about certain churches, elders, or saints, we praise them instead of giving thanks to God for them. If the situation in a certain church is good, it is because of God, not because of the church. Likewise, if a particular elder or saint is doing well, it also is because of God's grace. Therefore, instead of praising a church or a person, we should give thanks to God.

In mentioning petitions, prayers, intercessions, and thanksgivings, Paul's spirit was very burdened concerning the importance of prayer. He wanted his dear spiritual children to pray. Again and again I would emphasize the fact that we can have a proper church life only if we have a prayer life. I can testify that I have never prayed more than I have during the past several years. I can also testify that I have seen definite answers to my prayers. Recently, my activity was limited for a time so that I could rest and care for my health. When I heard about certain needs, I prayed for them. Perhaps the Lord limited me that He might impress me with the fact that prayer is more important than work. May we all learn the lesson that the way to have a good church life is to pray. This is crucial. If our talking is turned into praying, the church in our locality will be transformed.

When we pray in every place, we should lift up holy hands. Hands are a symbol of our doings. Hence, holy hands signify a holy living, a living sanctified and separated unto God. Such a holy life strengthens our prayer life. (*Life-study of 1 Timothy*, pp. 26, 28, 34)

*Further Reading: Life-study of 1 Timothy,* msgs. 3-4; *The Experience of Christ,* chs. 10, 23*

### *Enlightenment and inspiration:* _____

_____

_____

_____

## Morning Nourishment

Mal.     ...Take heed then to your spirit, and do not be
2:16     treacherous.
Rom.     For the mind set on the flesh is death, but the mind
8:6      set on the spirit is life and peace.
2 Cor.   I had no rest in my spirit, for I did not find Titus my
2:13     brother....

After you fan your spirit into flame, learn to practice another thing. Always manage your mind. Do not let your mind be a "wild horse." The mind is the great part of the soul, and the soul is in between our outward flesh and our inward spirit....After fanning our spirit into flame, we must learn to set our mind on the spirit [Rom. 8:6]. Our mind is very "talkative." The mind speaks to us everywhere at all times. If we do not control our mind, we can wander in our imagination all over the globe within a short time. We can dream in our mind even during the day. This is why we must direct our mind to the spirit. When we do this, we will sing to the Lord, praise the Lord, or speak forth the Lord.

We have to learn to fan our spirit into flame and to control our mind. Do not let the mind be set upon the flesh, but direct it to be set upon the spirit. This habit has to be built up in us. To set our mind on the flesh is death. To set our mind on the spirit is life and peace. (*The Spirit with Our Spirit,* pp. 84-85)

## Today's Reading

The way to know life and peace is by sensing life and peace....The first item of the sense of life is satisfaction. How do you know there is life within? There is satisfaction. You are satisfied and you sense the satisfaction. Then following satisfaction you have the sense of strengthening. When you are taking sides with the spirit, you also have the sense of refreshment. The sense of being watered is another sense of life. A person who is setting his mind on the spirit also senses enlightenment and the anointing (1 John 2:20, 27). The sense of life is the sense of satisfaction, strengthening, refreshing, watering, enlightenment, and anointing. When you sense all these items deep within, that is the sense of life, and this sense proves you are walking according to spirit.

To set the mind on the spirit is not only life but peace. The peace mentioned in Romans 8:6 is not the peace in our outward circumstances, but the peace within us. The sense of peace is firstly the sense of ease or comfort. Then following this there is harmony. There is no struggle or strife within. Rest, joy, and liberty are also included in the sense of peace. When you sense peace, you sense comfort, harmony, rest, joy, and liberty. These are the different aspects of the sense of peace. If we sense these things within us, this proves we are walking in the spirit.

Whenever you take sides with the flesh the result is death. You know death because you can sense it. You have the feeling, the consciousness of death. When you do things according to the flesh or according to your self you sense dissatisfaction and emptiness. Something within is also weakening you. This proves you are not in the spirit, but in the flesh or the soul. Oldness, dryness, darkness, and depression are other aspects of the sense of death versus the sense of life. Strife, discord, discomfort, restlessness, pain, bondage, and grief are aspects of the sense of death versus the sense of peace. When you have all these kinds of feelings, then you know where you are—you are in death. Don't argue or reason. Even if what you are doing is good and "holy" you must check with your inner feeling. Do you have the ease, harmony, rest, comfort, joy, or liberty?

If you have these positive inward registrations and feelings, this proves you are in the spirit. If you don't have these kinds of feelings, regardless of how holy, how good, and how scriptural you consider a course of action to be, you are not in the spirit, but in the self, in the flesh. The Christian life is a life absolutely according to the spirit. It is not according to any reasons, any teachings, or any standard of right or wrong, good or bad, worldly or holy. Our Christian life is according to spirit, and we know the spirit by the inner sense of life and peace. (*Our Human Spirit,* pp. 66-68)

*Further Reading: The Spirit with Our Spirit,* ch. 8; *Our Human Spirit,* ch. 9

### *Enlightenment and inspiration:* _____

_____

_____

_____

## Morning Nourishment

Heb.  For the word of God is living and operative and
4:12  sharper than any two-edged sword, and piercing
      even to the dividing of soul and spirit,...and able to
      discern the thoughts and intentions of the heart.
Matt.  For whoever wants to save his soul-life shall lose it; but
16:25  whoever loses his soul-life for My sake shall find it.
2 Tim.  But flee youthful lusts, and pursue righteousness,
2:22   faith, love, peace with those who call on the Lord out
       of a pure heart.

We can live the normal church life and overcome the church's degradation by exercising our regenerated spirit of power, love, and sobermindedness (2 Tim. 1:7). We have to fan our spirit into flame (v. 6). Our spirit of sobermindedness and power also needs to be of love. We will not let anyone go or give up on anyone when we exercise such a forgiving and loving spirit.

In order to overcome the degradation of the church, we must enjoy the Lord in our spirit as the abiding grace. Christ today is the life-giving Spirit indwelling our spirit. Second Timothy 4:22, the last verse of this Epistle, says, "The Lord be with your spirit. Grace be with you." Thus, the end of this Epistle on how to deal with the degradation of the church is that we must enjoy Christ in our spirit as our abiding grace. This is the way to live the church life in the vital groups under the degradation of the church. (*The Vital Groups*, p. 11)

## Today's Reading

Hebrews 4:12...says that the word of God can divide our soul from our spirit and is able to *discern* the thoughts and intentions of the heart. Quite often our thoughts are deceiving. But if we exercise our spirit, there is a discernment that our thoughts are evil, because behind our thoughts there is an evil intention. To discern the thoughts and intents of the heart equals the dividing of the soul from the spirit. All the time you have to keep your spirit separate from your soul. The enemy's strategy is always to mix our spirit up with our soul. In today's world nearly everyone is in a mixed situation. They mix up their spirit with their soul. Whenever such mixing is there, the spirit loses and the soul wins.

Before a brother begins to talk to his wife about another brother, he has to consider, "Is this of my spirit or of my soul?" If it is of his soul, what he says will be either gossip or criticism. If it is of his spirit, what he says will be something led by the Lord. This shows that we have to discern our spirit from our soul. We, the ones who are seeking after Christ, must learn to fan our spirit into flame, to set our mind on the spirit, and also to discern our spirit from our soul.

Our God-given spirit is our capital and our capacity. We have to use our spirit, to employ our spirit, and to exercise our spirit by fanning it into flame, by setting our mind upon it, and by discerning it from our soul. Of course, it is easy to know what is of the flesh and what is of the spirit; but quite often it is a very mixed-up situation between what is of the soul and what is of the spirit. This is why we have to discern.

Our Christian walk is a very fine walk. If we are going to walk according to our spirit, we must learn not to do things too fast or to say things too quickly. It is safe to wait awhile....To wait in this way helps us to walk according to our spirit.

The battle in the Christian life is always there. Even within us there is a battle between the spirit and the flesh and even the more between the spirit and the soul. So we have to exercise our spirit, to use our spirit, that is, to fan our spirit into flame. Then we should learn how to control our mind by setting our mind upon our spirit. We should also always discern what is of the spirit and what is of the soul. If something is not of the spirit, we do not want to say it or do it. This is to use, to exercise, our spirit. I hope we will practice using our spirit until we build up a strong habit of exercising our spirit. (*The Spirit with Our Spirit*, pp. 85-86)

*Further Reading: The Vital Groups,* msg. 1; *The Spirit with Our Spirit,* ch. 8; *Life-study of Song of Songs,* msg. 5

### *Enlightenment and inspiration:* _____

_____

_____

_____

## *Hymns,* #866

1  Exercise the spirit!
   Human thought reject;
   Meet with one another,
   Body life respect.

2  Exercise the spirit!
   All the forms forsake;
   Share with one another,
   Each of Christ partake.

3  Exercise the spirit!
   Natural sense renounce;
   Serve with one another,
   Christ the Lord announce.

4  Exercise the spirit!
   Soulish life deny;
   Helping one another,
   On the Lord rely.

5  Freed within the spirit
   From self-righteousness,
   From self-condemnation
   And self-consciousness.

6  Freed within the spirit
   From self-will and pride,
   From self-love and glory,
   All to override.

7  Exercise the spirit,
   Victory to claim
   By the blood which cleanses
   And the mighty Name.

8  Exercise the spirit
   Thus to touch the Lord;
   Ever by the spirit
   Take Him thru His Word.

9  It is by the spirit
   Christ is testified;
   It is by the spirit
   Man is satisfied.

10 Exercise the spirit!
   This is what we need!
   Exercise the spirit!
   May the Lord so lead!

*Composition for prophecy with main point and sub-points:* _____

_____

_____

_____

_____

_____

_____

_____

_____

_____

_____

_____

_____

_____

_____

_____

_____

_____

_____

_____

_____

_____

_____

_____

_____

_____

_____

_____

_____

_____

_____

_____

_____

_____

_____

_____

_____

_____

_____

### *The Basic Factor of the Decline—*
### *Turning Away from Paul's Completing Ministry*

Scripture Reading: 2 Tim. 1:12-18; 1 Tim. 1:3-4; 6:3-4

*Day 1*

I. **The Lord's recovery today is the recovery of the central vision of Paul's completing ministry; this is the vision of the age in the ministry of the age (Col. 1:25; cf. Acts 9:4-5, 15; 22:14-15; 26:16-19):**

A. In the New Testament the apostles, especially the apostle Paul, completed the word of God, the divine revelation, regarding God in us as our contents, Christ as the mystery of God, and the church as the mystery of Christ, thereby giving us a full revelation of God's economy (Eph. 3:9; 2 Cor. 4:7; Col. 2:2; Eph. 3:4).

B. The goal of the Lord's recovery is the completion of the word of God, which is the commission of the age (Acts 26:18-19):

1. We need to complete the word of God in the sense of fully preaching the word, declaring all the counsel of God, all of God's economy, so that we may present every man full-grown in Christ (20:26-27; Col. 1:28-29).

2. We need to complete the word of God in the sense of experiencing Christ subjectively to enjoy Him in our daily living so that the proper church life may come forth to be the corporate manifestation of God in the flesh, the great mystery of godliness (Phil. 1:19-21a; Eph. 3:16-21; 1 Tim. 3:15-16a).

*Day 2*

II. **The basic factor of the decline and apostasy of the church is the turning away from Paul's completing ministry (2 Tim. 1:15; cf. 2:17-18; 4:4, 10, 14-16):**

A. For all those in Asia to turn away from Paul meant that they turned away not from his person but from his ministry centered on the economy of God

(1:15-17; 4:4; 1 Tim. 1:3-4; Eph. 3:2, 8-11, 16-21; Col. 1:25; 1 Cor. 9:17).

B. Among the seven churches in Asia was the church in Ephesus, which was fully established by Paul's ministry (Acts 19:1-20; 20:17-38; Eph. 1:1; 1 Tim. 1:3-4).

C. About thirty years after Paul said that all who were in Asia had turned away from him, the Lord used John to speak to the churches in Asia in the stage of His intensification (Rev. 1:4; 3:1; 4:5; 5:6).

D. Because they turned away from Paul's ministry, the churches in Asia declined into degradation; the first letter being written to the church in Ephesus proves that they took the lead to forsake Paul's ministry and teaching (2:1-7; cf. 3:16).

E. The church in Ephesus left their first love because they left Paul's ministry (Eph. 1:4; 3:16-19; 4:2, 15-16; 5:2; 6:24; Rev. 2:4).

*Day 3*

F. The striking point of the churches' degradation was the teaching of Balaam (v. 14), the teaching of the Nicolaitans (v. 15), and the teaching of Jezebel (v. 20); these different teachings crept in because the churches turned away from Paul's teaching, the unique teaching of God's eternal economy:

1. Different teachings separate us from the genuine appreciation, love, and enjoyment of the precious person of the Lord Jesus Christ Himself as our life and our everything (2 Cor. 11:2-3).

2. Teachings that differ from the healthy words of the Lord always issue from people's pride and self-conceit, which blind them (1 Tim. 6:3-4).

G. One church in Asia was unique and highly appraised by the Lord—the church in Philadelphia; the Lord appreciated them because they kept the word, which means they did not turn away from the healthy teaching of God's economy, the teaching according to godliness (Rev. 3:8; 1 Tim. 1:10; 6:3; 2 Tim. 4:3).

H. The ministry of the healthy, living words of the Lord always brings forth godliness—a life that lives Christ and expresses God in Christ (1 Tim. 6:3; 2 Tim. 1:13; Matt. 4:4; John 6:57, 63; Rev. 2:7).

*Day 4*  III. **Whether or not a particular ministry is part of the New Testament ministry can be proved by applying three governing principles: the principle of the processed Triune God being dispensed into His chosen people; the principle of Christ and the church; and the principle of Christ, the Spirit, life, and the church (1 Cor. 1:10; cf. 14:8):**

A. If your teaching can pass this threefold test, your teaching is a part of the New Testament ministry, the ministry of the age (1:10; cf. 14:8).

B. The leadership in the New Testament ministry is the leadership of the controlling, God-given revelation of God's economy (Acts 26:19; Prov. 29:18):

1. You should not do a work to attract people to follow you; such a one who makes himself attractive is wrong, and if you are attracted to follow him, you help him to be wrong, destroying yourself and him (cf. 2 Cor. 4:5).

2. In the Lord's work we should beware of the ambition to get a place or a district for our work, captivating people to be our private co-workers; our fallen disposition by birth likes to captivate people (1 Cor. 11:19; Gal. 5:20).

3. We should never follow any person; we should simply follow the Lord according to the heavenly and consummate vision of the age (Acts 26:19).

C. The saints who have been raised up by this ministry have a taste for this ministry; this taste is the controlling factor in the Lord's recovery (1 Pet. 2:3).

D. Those who have been raised with this taste will reject a taste that is contrary to it; this means that if you speak something contrary to the taste of the

Lord's recovery, your speaking will be rejected, and you will suffer loss.

*Day 5*  **IV. There are two secrets of discerning the genuine New Testament ministry:**

A. The genuine ministry stirs up our love for the Lord Jesus as our Bridegroom so that we may enjoy Him to the uttermost as our Husband (2 Cor. 11:2-3).

B. The genuine ministry strengthens us to follow Christ in the fellowship of His sufferings for the sake of His Body (vv. 23-33; Col. 1:25; cf. 2 Tim. 2:12, 16-18).

*Day 6*  **V. In order to be preserved in the Lord's recovery, we must "guard the good deposit through the Holy Spirit who dwells in us" (1:14):**

A. According to verse 13, the deposit must refer to the deposit of the healthy words of God's economy, including the riches of life in the Lord's words, which He has stored in us; we have to deposit the Lord's healthy words into our being, like we deposit money in a bank (1 Tim. 6:20; Col. 3:16; Psa. 119:72):

1. To hold a pattern of the healthy words means to live by the healthy words, being nourished with the words of the full gospel concerning God's New Testament economy and the sweet words that contain and convey the riches of Christ (2 Tim. 1:13; 1 Tim. 4:6).

2. If we are persons acting, behaving, and having our life in the Spirit through the exercise of our spirit, all that has been deposited in our being will be guarded through the Spirit who is indwelling us (2 Tim. 1:12, 14).

B. In a darkened and confused situation, we must cleave to the enlightening and ordering word in the New Testament, the healthy teaching of God's economy, which concerns God's dispensing of Himself in His Divine Trinity into His chosen people so that they may be constituted into the Body of Christ for the manifestation of the Triune God (Titus 1:9; Acts 2:42; 1 Tim. 1:3-4).

## *Morning Nourishment*

Col. Of which I became a minister according to the
1:25-26 stewardship of God, which was given to me for you,
to complete the word of God, the mystery which has
been hidden from the ages and from the genera-
tions but now has been manifested to His saints.
28-29 Whom we announce, admonishing every man and
teaching every man in all wisdom that we may
present every man full-grown in Christ; for which
also I labor, struggling according to His operation
which operates in me in power.

Paul's intention in the book of Colossians is to complete the
word of God. This was his main purpose in writing this Epistle.
[Colossians 1:25 and 26]...indicate that the word of God completed by Paul is the mystery now manifested to the saints. Furthermore, according to verse 27, this mystery is Christ in us, the
hope of glory. The goal of this mystery is to produce the church.

At the time the book of Colossians was written, Judaism had
been in existence for centuries, and the church had come into being. Nevertheless, even though the church had come into being,
the word of God had not yet been completed. Paul was troubled
by the situation at Colosse. The Jewish and Gentile believers
were neglecting Christ and the church; they were focusing their
attention on such things as Judaistic observances and heathen
philosophy. Many people, Jews and Christians alike, claimed to
know God and to worship Him. However, Christ was being neglected and the genuine church life was being set aside. Therefore, Paul wrote the Epistle to the Colossians in order to
complete the word of God. (*Life-study of Colossians,* p. 266)

## *Today's Reading*

In principle, the situation today is the same as that in Colosse
at the time Paul wrote to the Colossians. Judaism and Christianity have been on earth for centuries. Although the Jews have
the Old Testament and the Christians have the entire Bible,

very few people truly are experiencing Christ for the proper church life. Christ is still neglected, and the church life is still ignored. Hence, there is still the need for the word of God to be completed in a practical way.

What is the completion of the word of God, the completion of the divine revelation? In simple terms, to complete the word of God is to experience Christ subjectively and to enjoy Him in our daily living so that the proper church life may come forth to express God. This revelation is the completion of the word of God.

Christians today are involved in many different kinds of work for the Lord. But where is the experience of Christ, and where is the practice of the church life? Paul knew that neither Judaism nor any other religion could fulfill the desire of God's heart. God's desire is to have the church life produced through His people's personal experience of Christ. God wants an organism, the Body of Christ, brought forth through the experience of Christ. At the time of Paul, there were many Jews and a good number of Christians as well. But as Paul considered the situation, he could have asked, "Where is the experience of Christ, and where is the church to fulfill the desire of God's heart?" We should ask the same questions today.

We need to admit that we ourselves are short of the experience of Christ. We have been enlightened to see that God does not want anything other than Christ for the church life. However, in our experience we are still short of Christ. This means that, in a very practical sense, we also are short of the completion of the word of God. We lack Christ for the producing of the church. We know that only one thing matters—Christ for the church. However, we are still short of Christ. Before we can minister Christ to others, we need to minister Him to ourselves. (*Life-study of Colossians*, pp. 266-267)

*Further Reading: Life-study of Colossians*, msgs. 11, 13, 16, 32; *The Completing Ministry of Paul*, chs. 1, 10-12; *Life-study of Acts*, msgs. 25-26

***Enlightenment and inspiration:*** _____

_____

_____

_____

*Morning Nourishment*

2 Tim.  This you know, that all who are in Asia turned away
1:15  from me, of whom are Phygelus and Hermogenes.
Rev.  But I have *one thing* against you, that you have left
2:4  your first love.
3:16  So, because you are lukewarm and neither hot nor
cold, I am about to spew you out of My mouth.

The reason that the church in Ephesus degraded was that it
had taken the lead to depart from the teaching of the apostles.
To depart from the apostles' teaching is to depart from the apostles' vision. With the departure of the apostles' teaching came
the teaching of Balaam (Rev. 2:14), the teaching of the
Nicolaitans (vv. 6, 15), and the teaching of Jezebel (v. 20). These
three teachings represent all the heresies in Christianity.

Paul tells us in Colossians that the ministry he received from
God was to complete the word of God (1:25). After Paul com-
pleted his ministry and finished his Epistles, the church in
Ephesus took the lead to bring all the churches in Asia away
from the teaching of the apostle Paul. By the time the book of
Revelation was written, we find the apostle John continuing the
Lord's commission and following Paul in fulfilling his ministry.
John continued from where Paul had left off in his ministry.
While Paul was on earth, he dealt with the problem of decline.
The last church he dealt with was Ephesus in Asia. Thirty years
later, at the beginning of the book of Revelation, in writing to the
seven churches in Asia, the first church that was addressed was
the church in Ephesus. John rebuked Ephesus for having left its
first love. The reason it had left its first love is that it had left the
apostles' teaching. (*The Vision of the Age*, pp. 46-47)

## *Today's Reading*

When Paul said that all who were in Asia turned away from
him, this does not indicate that they turned away from the person of Paul because the person of Paul was far away from them
[in Rome]. This verse indicates that they all turned away from
Paul's ministry. Among the churches in Asia was the church in

Ephesus, which was fully established by Paul's ministry as recorded in Acts 19. They received the gospel, the teaching, the edification, and the establishment from the ministry of the apostle Paul. But by the time Paul was imprisoned in Rome, they had all turned away from his ministry.

About thirty years later, the Lord used John to continue His divine revelation. The Lord came back to all the churches in Asia who had turned away from Paul. Because they turned away from Paul's ministry, the churches in Asia declined into a situation full of degradation. The degradation of the churches in Asia as recorded in Revelation 2 and 3 was due to their turning away from the proper ministry. This degradation began with their losing of the first love toward the Lord, which transpired at Ephesus (2:4), and ended with the lukewarmness (3:16), the Christlessness. The Lord as the Head of the church is standing outside the degraded church, knocking at her door (3:20). (*Elders' Training, Book 7: One Accord for the Lord's Move*, p. 116)

In his Epistles, especially in 2 Timothy, Paul spoke thoroughly concerning the degradation of the church. He said that all who were in Asia turned away from him (2 Tim. 1:15)....They turned away from his New Testament ministry, the apostles' teaching which he preached. All that Paul had preached to them, all that he had nurtured them with, all that he had taught them, and all that he had shown them were completely abandoned by them. The first thing that happened in the degradation of the church was the turning away from the apostles' teaching. If all of us today in the Lord's recovery did not care for the apostles' teaching preached by Brother Watchman Nee and me, the church and the Lord's recovery would become degraded. To remain in the apostles' teaching is a tremendous grace. (*How to Be a Co-worker and an Elder and How to Fulfill Their Obligations*, p. 44)

*Further Reading: The Vision of the Age*, chs. 2-3; *Elders' Training, Book 7: One Accord for the Lord's Move*, ch. 8; *How to Be a Co-worker and an Elder and How to Fulfill Their Obligations*, ch. 3

*Enlightenment and inspiration:* _____

_____

_____

_____

### *Morning Nourishment*

1 Tim. If anyone teaches different things and does not con-
6:3-4 sent to healthy words, those of our Lord Jesus Christ,
and the teaching which is according to godliness, he is
blinded with pride, understanding nothing, but is diseased with questionings and contentions of words, out
of which come envy, strife, slanders, evil suspicions.
Rev. I know your works; behold, I have put before you an
3:8 opened door which no one can shut, because you
have a little power and have kept My word and have
not denied My name.

In [the] seven epistles in Revelation 2 and 3, the striking point
of the churches' degradation was three kinds of teachings: the
teaching of Balaam, a Gentile prophet (2:14), the teaching of
the Nicolaitans to build the hierarchy (2:15), and the teaching
of the woman, the so-called prophetess, Jezebel, full of heresies
and fornication (2:20). These three kinds of teachings crept in
because they left the teaching of the apostle. Why has Christianity become degraded? Because they turned away from the apostle's teaching. Thus, all the different teachings came in.

In 1 Timothy 1:3 and 6:3 Paul warned not to teach different
things. The saints should teach according to Paul's teaching. Those
in Asia definitely turned away from Paul's teaching, and the result...was that they received three kinds of heretical teachings.
The teaching of Balaam to worship the idols, the teaching of the
Nicolaitans to build up the hierarchy, even the papal system, and
the teaching of Jezebel to bring the leaven of evil, heretical, and
pagan things into the fine flour of Christ (Matt. 13:33) came in because the proper teaching was rejected. Within thirty years after
Paul's final Epistle to Timothy, these churches had reached such a
point of degradation. It is dangerous to leave or turn away from
the apostle's teaching, from the apostle's proper revelation. (*Elders'
Training, Book 7: One Accord for the Lord's Move*, pp. 116-117)

### *Today's Reading*

The Lord came in these seven epistles to judge those degraded churches. His eyes were as a flame of fire (Rev. 1:14) to observe, search, and enlighten, and out of His mouth proceeded a sharp two-edged sword (1:16), which is His discerning, judging, and slaying word (Heb. 4:12; Eph. 6:17). They turned away from the right word, so the Lord came with this word to judge them. The Lord's feet were like shining brass, as having been fired in a furnace (Rev. 1:15). Brass signifies divine judgment (Exo. 27:1-6). The Lord's coming to the churches in such a way fit in with their turning away from the apostle's teaching and their picking up of different teachings.

One church was unique, and was highly appraised by the Lord—the church in Philadelphia. The Lord highly appraised them and even appreciated them because they kept the word (Rev. 3:8). That means they did not turn away from the apostle's proper teaching. Although they were weak, the Lord still appraised them highly, telling them that they had a little power and that they had kept the word.

To turn away from the proper teaching is a terrible thing that will result in degradation and in picking up other teachings. I say this as a warning to those dear ones who would not take the new way. To reject the proper revelation, the proper teaching, of the leaders among you is a dangerous thing. You will open the door for other teachings to come in and suffer degradation. I hope that all of the church people in the recovery would not be followers of those in Asia who turned away from Paul's ministry. Rather, I hope we would follow the pattern of the church in Philadelphia—keeping the Lord's word even though we only have a little strength. Let us keep the word of the Lord, which is to remain in the teachings of the apostle, to remain in the healthy words, to remain in the unique revelation from the Lord with the proper leadership. Then we are safe. (*Elders' Training, Book 7: One Accord for the Lord's Move*, pp. 117-118)

*Further Reading: Elders' Training, Book 7: One Accord for the Lord's Move*, ch. 8

***Enlightenment and inspiration:*** _____

_____
_____
_____

## *Morning Nourishment*

1 Cor. Now I beseech you, brothers, through the name of our
1:10  Lord Jesus Christ, that you all speak the same thing
and *that* there be no divisions among you, but *that* you
be attuned in the same mind and in the same opinion.

15:45 ...The last Adam *became* a life-giving Spirit.

Eph. This mystery is great, but I speak with regard to
5:32  Christ and the church.

The first principle we have seen [in our interpretation of the
Bible] is a general principle—the Triune God dispensing Himself
into His chosen people. The second principle is in more detail—
with Christ for the church. Now we see a third principle of Christ,
the Spirit, life, and the church. Any message or any development
of the Bible without Christ, the Spirit, life, and the church is an
empty shell with no content. The content of the Bible is Christ,
the Spirit, life, and the church. At least one of these items must be
present in your development of the truth. Also, in your preaching
of the gospel at least one of these items should be present. I saw
some evangelists in China who preached quite prevailingly, but in
their gospel they did not preach much reality of Christ, the Spirit,
life, and the church. Their prevailing evangelical work attracted a
good number of people. However, many of these people turned to
the way of the Lord's recovery to pick up Christ, the Spirit, life,
and the church. They all remained and became very useful to the
Lord's interest. Those who did not turn this way, including the
evangelists, either disappeared or still remained with emptiness....The ones who turned this way not only remained but they
became solid with the truth concerning Christ, the Spirit, life, and
the church. (*Elders' Training, Book 3: The Way to Carry Out the
Vision,* p. 65)

## *Today's Reading*

You must develop the biblical truth in the way of Christ, the
Spirit, life, and the church. Even if you have a good portion of the
Word with a good idea to stir up people's interest, you must con-
sider whether or not Christ, the Spirit, life, and the church are the

content of your message. If they are not the content, you should forget about it. Do not go further to develop anything apart from this governing principle because you will waste your time. Also, you will have no safeguard and you will be led astray.

All the heresies came in by the way of developing the truth in the Bible apart from Christ, the Spirit, life, and the church. Any doctrine developed apart from these four items will issue in heresy or division....Some even developed the doctrine of holiness apart from Christ, the Spirit, life, and the church. We, however, should develop the doctrine of holiness with Christ for the church. We need to tell people that holiness is Christ Himself, and this Christ today is the life-giving Spirit (1 Cor. 15:45). Not only is His Spirit called the Holy Spirit, but also He is called the life-giving Spirit who imparts the divine life into us for our sanctification. Holiness is God's nature and is related to life. If you do not have God's life, you do not have God's nature, which is holiness. If God's holiness is going to be increased within you, you must live according to God's nature and by God's life. We must also realize that this holy life should not only be for our personal living but it must also be a part of the church life. If we would develop the doctrine of holiness with Christ, with the Spirit, with life, and with the church, we would see a marvelous revelation. Otherwise, a holiness sect will be created. This is why some have established holiness churches. These are actually holiness divisions cutting the Body into pieces.

Always remember these three intrinsic principles of developing the truth in the Bible: the Triune God dispensing Himself into His chosen and redeemed people; Christ and the church; and Christ, the Spirit, life, and the church. (*Elders' Training, Book 3: The Way to Carry Out the Vision*, pp. 66-67)

*Further Reading: Elders' Training, Book 3: The Way to Carry Out the Vision*, chs. 4-6, 10, 12; *Elders' Training, Book 1: The Ministry of the New Testament*, ch. 1; *A Word of Love to the Co-workers, Elders, Lovers, and Seekers of the Lord*, chs. 3-4

*Enlightenment and inspiration:* _____
_____
_____
_____

## *Morning Nourishment*

2 Cor.  For I am jealous over you with a jealousy of God; for
11:2-3  I betrothed you to one husband to present *you as*
        a pure virgin to Christ. But I fear lest somehow, as
        the serpent deceived Eve by his craftiness, your
        thoughts would be corrupted from the simplicity and
        the purity toward Christ.
Col.    I now rejoice in my sufferings on your behalf and fill
1:24    up on my part that which is lacking of the afflictions of
        Christ in my flesh for His Body, which is the church.

In 2 Corinthians 11 we have two secrets of discerning the genuine
from the false: enjoying the Lord as our life supply and suffering in
following the Lord. On the one hand, we enjoy the Lord Jesus; on the
other hand, we follow Him to live a life of suffering. This enjoyment
and suffering are determining factors by which we may discern
what is genuine and what is false. Anything that helps us to enjoy
the Lord and that strengthens us to follow Him in His suffering is
genuine. What does not encourage us in these two matters is false.

At the beginning of chapter eleven Paul speaks of the Lord as
our dear Husband. Toward the end of this chapter he refers to the
churches. The first secret of discernment is related to the enjoyment of Christ as our Husband; the second is related to the proper
concern and care for all the churches, a concern that involves fill-
ing up the lack of the sufferings of Christ for the Body.... We need
to enjoy Him as our Husband, loving Him with a pure and single
heart and having a mind that is not corrupted by the deceiver. We
also thank Him for showing us that we need to follow in His foot-
steps and be willing to suffer what He suffered for the building up
of the church, His Body. (*Life-study of 2 Corinthians,* pp. 479-480)

### *Today's Reading*

Because Paul was wise, he did not argue with the Judaizers
concerning doctrine. Instead, he told the Corinthians that he was
jealous over them with a jealousy of God. He went on to say that
he had betrothed them to one husband in order to present a pure
virgin to Christ. What a wonderful way of speaking! Paul's word

in verse 2 is very touching. It touches our heart in a deep way and stirs up our love for the Lord Jesus. Very often the Life-study messages touch our hearts in the same way. After reading a few pages of a message, the tender feeling within you for the Lord Jesus is stirred up, and you realize afresh how dear and precious He is.

Today's Judaizers seek to shake the believers away from simply loving the Lord Jesus. Nevertheless, we should turn from the Mosaic law and from the prophets and focus our attention on the Lord. We need to see from 11:2 that we have been betrothed to one husband in order to be presented as a pure virgin to Christ. Therefore, we should say, "Our dear Lord Jesus is our unique Husband, and I am part of His virgin. I don't care for doctrine or theology. I care only for the ministry that ministers Christ to me. He is the pleasant and dear One whom I love."

The best way to discern a matter is to discern according to life or death. We need to ask questions like this: Does this teaching help me to enjoy the Lord more and bring me into life, or does it cause the poison of death to be injected into me? You may find that if you accept a certain kind of teaching or preaching, taking it into you, immediately your inward enjoyment of the Lord is cut off. Some things function like insulation that stops the flowing of the divine electricity. Therefore, we must learn to discern, to differentiate, matters by life and death.

The secret of real discernment...is to discern a preaching or teaching by whether or not it helps us to enjoy the Lord and gain more life supply. If anyone's preaching cuts us off from the enjoyment of the Lord, that preaching must be of the serpent, of Satan. But if someone's preaching helps us to enjoy the Lord, that preaching is of God. Therefore,...we need to discern according to death or life. Many of those who have left the Lord's recovery have neither the life supply nor the enjoyment. This is an indication that they have taken in something that is not of the Lord. (*Life-study of 2 Corinthians,* pp. 462-463, 469-470)

*Further Reading: Life-study of 2 Corinthians,* msgs. 52-54

***Enlightenment and inspiration:*** _____

_____

_____
_____

## Morning Nourishment

**2 Tim. 1:12-14** For which cause also I suffer these things; but I am not ashamed, for I know whom I have believed, and I am persuaded that He is able to guard my deposit unto that day. Hold a pattern of the healthy words that you have heard from me, in the faith and love which are in Christ Jesus. Guard the good deposit through the Holy Spirit who dwells in us.

In 2 Timothy 1:14 the Spirit is also dwelling in the believers through whom they guard the good deposit. Since we were saved we have received many things from God into us as a kind of deposit....Within us and especially within our spirit, we have a divine deposit. God's life, God's Spirit, and all the precious truths we have seen in the Lord's recovery have been deposited into our being. How can we safeguard this deposit? It is only through the Holy Spirit who dwells in us. If we are a person acting, behaving, and having our life in the Spirit, all that has been deposited into our being will be guarded. If we forget about the Spirit and walk in our flesh and according to our mentality, we will immediately be the same as the nations who are apart from God (Eph. 4:17-18). If this were the case, there would be no safeguarding of the good things deposited in our being. We need to safeguard the good deposit by the Spirit. (*God's New Testament Economy*, p. 180)

## Today's Reading

[In 2 Timothy 1:13] a pattern of healthy words is an example. The word in verse 12 is a pattern, an example, of healthy words. To hold a pattern of healthy words means to live by the healthy words. Paul's intention in this section was to encourage and strengthen Timothy to not live in cooperation with the degradation but to live in another way. To live another way, in spite of the degradation of the church, is to be nourished with the healthy words. Then you yourself, your living, and your daily life will be a pattern of the healthy words.

Now we have to apply this to our own experience. We should not just pass on these crucial points to others. Rather we should live these crucial points in spite of the environment of this age, in spite of the trend of today's Christianity, and even in spite of the world situation. Today's world situation is altogether concerning how to become rich, yet we should live in another way. This other way is to all the time be nourished with the healthy words. Then we will hold the healthy words in our living as a pattern. Paul was such a person. Paul lived such a pattern in front of Timothy. Therefore, Paul charged him to keep this pattern. All the saints should hold a pattern of the healthy words. (*Elders' Training, Book 6: The Crucial Points of the Truth in Paul's Epistles*, p. 118)

Before Paul's second imprisonment, there were many Jews among the churches in the Gentile lands who were beginning to teach Old Testament things different from the New Testament teaching. By the time Paul went into prison, the Judaizing Christians had become even more aggressive....Paul's imprisonment gave the Judaizing Christians and those who taught differently a strong ground to speak [against his teachings]. This is the reason Paul wrote the second Epistle to Timothy.

In 2 Timothy 1:13...Paul reminded Timothy to hold "the healthy words." He had already spoken about this in 1 Timothy 6. As we have already seen, these healthy words are the words of the Lord Jesus in the New Testament plus the preaching of the Lord's apostles....Paul charged Timothy to hold these words. This proves that at that time some believers were already not holding these words. This is a very serious matter.

Second Timothy 1:14 says, "Guard the good deposit through the Holy Spirit who dwells in us." This is the Lord's commission to the apostles. It is also the apostles' charge to the believers. We have to deposit the Lord's healthy words, including the riches of life in the Lord's words, into our being, like we deposit money in the bank. (*The Vision of the Age*, pp. 64-65)

*Further Reading: God's New Testament Economy*, ch. 16; *Elders' Training, Book 6: The Crucial Points of the Truth in Paul's Epistles,* ch. 9; *The Vision of the Age*, ch. 3; *Life-study of 2 Timothy*, msg. 2

*Enlightenment and inspiration:* _____

_____

_____

_____

### *Hymns,* #549

1    Enter the veil and go without the camp,
     Taste heaven's sweetness, thus the earth
          forsake;
     If by the Holiest I am satisfied,
     How can I of earth's vanities partake?


2    Enter the veil and go without the camp,
     By heaven's presence will the earth depart;
     If heaven's glory doth my spirit charm,
     How can earth's happiness possess my heart?


3    Enter the veil, behold the glorious Christ,
     Go out the camp to Jesus, let Him lead;
     If throne and crown my spirit here enthrall,
     Manger and cross cannot my steps impede.


4    Enter the veil for resurrection pow'r,
     Go out the camp to bear the cross and woe,
     If I His radiant face in heaven see,
     His footsteps I will follow here below.


5    Enter the veil, on heaven's fatness feast,
     Without the camp, in hardship persevere;
     Though earthly trials sorely pain my heart,
     Heaven's communion doth my spirit cheer.


6    Enter the veil, Christ's riches there enjoy,
     Without the camp, the needs of men supply;
     The life of heaven living out thru me
     The souls of earth will bless and satisfy.


7    Enter the veil till it exists no more,
     Go out the camp till all the camps are gone;
     Until the heavens and the earth unite,
     Till God and man together dwell in one.

*Composition for prophecy with main point and sub-points:* _____

_____

_____

_____

_____

_____

_____

_____

_____

_____

_____

_____

_____

_____

_____

_____

_____

_____

_____

_____

_____

_____

_____

_____

_____

_____

_____

_____

_____

_____

_____

_____

_____

_____

_____

# Reading Schedule for the Recovery Version of the New Testament with Footnotes

| Wk. | Lord's Day | Monday | Tuesday | Wednesday | Thursday | Friday | Saturday |
|---|---|---|---|---|---|---|---|
| 1 | ☐ Matt 1:1-2 | ☐ 1:3-7 | ☐ 1:8-17 | ☐ 1:18-25 | ☐ 2:1-23 | ☐ 3:1-6 | ☐ 3:7-17 |
| 2 | ☐ 4:1-11 | ☐ 4:12-25 | ☐ 5:1-4 | ☐ 5:5-12 | ☐ 5:13-20 | ☐ 5:21-26 | ☐ 5:27-48 |
| 3 | ☐ 6:1-8 | ☐ 6:9-18 | ☐ 6:19-34 | ☐ 7:1-12 | ☐ 7:13-29 | ☐ 8:1-13 | ☐ 8:14-22 |
| 4 | ☐ 8:23-34 | ☐ 9:1-13 | ☐ 9:14-17 | ☐ 9:18-34 | ☐ 9:35—10:5 | ☐ 10:6-25 | ☐ 10:26-42 |
| 5 | ☐ 11:1-15 | ☐ 11:16-30 | ☐ 12:1-14 | ☐ 12:15-32 | ☐ 12:33-42 | ☐ 12:43—13:2 | ☐ 13:3-12 |
| 6 | ☐ 13:13-30 | ☐ 13:31-43 | ☐ 13:44-58 | ☐ 14:1-13 | ☐ 14:14-21 | ☐ 14:22-36 | ☐ 15:1-20 |
| 7 | ☐ 15:21-31 | ☐ 15:32-39 | ☐ 16:1-12 | ☐ 16:13-20 | ☐ 16:21-28 | ☐ 17:1-13 | ☐ 17:14-27 |
| 8 | ☐ 18:1-14 | ☐ 18:15-22 | ☐ 18:23-35 | ☐ 19:1-15 | ☐ 19:16-30 | ☐ 20:1-16 | ☐ 20:17-34 |
| 9 | ☐ 21:1-11 | ☐ 21:12-22 | ☐ 21:23-32 | ☐ 21:33-46 | ☐ 22:1-22 | ☐ 22:23-33 | ☐ 22:34-46 |
| 10 | ☐ 23:1-12 | ☐ 23:13-39 | ☐ 24:1-14 | ☐ 24:15-31 | ☐ 24:32-51 | ☐ 25:1-13 | ☐ 25:14-30 |
| 11 | ☐ 25:31-46 | ☐ 26:1-16 | ☐ 26:17-35 | ☐ 26:36-46 | ☐ 26:47-64 | ☐ 26:65-75 | ☐ 27:1-26 |
| 12 | ☐ 27:27-44 | ☐ 27:45-56 | ☐ 27:57—28:15 | ☐ 28:16-20 | ☐ Mark 1:1 | ☐ 1:2-6 | ☐ 1:7-13 |
| 13 | ☐ 1:14-28 | ☐ 1:29-45 | ☐ 2:1-12 | ☐ 2:13-28 | ☐ 3:1-19 | ☐ 3:20-35 | ☐ 4:1-25 |
| 14 | ☐ 4:26-41 | ☐ 5:1-20 | ☐ 5:21-43 | ☐ 6:1-29 | ☐ 6:30-56 | ☐ 7:1-23 | ☐ 7:24-37 |
| 15 | ☐ 8:1-26 | ☐ 8:27—9:1 | ☐ 9:2-29 | ☐ 9:30-50 | ☐ 10:1-16 | ☐ 10:17-34 | ☐ 10:35-52 |
| 16 | ☐ 11:1-16 | ☐ 11:17-33 | ☐ 12:1-27 | ☐ 12:28-44 | ☐ 13:1-13 | ☐ 13:14-37 | ☐ 14:1-26 |
| 17 | ☐ 14:27-52 | ☐ 14:53-72 | ☐ 15:1-15 | ☐ 15:16-47 | ☐ 16:1-8 | ☐ 16:9-20 | ☐ Luke 1:1-4 |
| 18 | ☐ 1:5-25 | ☐ 1:26-46 | ☐ 1:47-56 | ☐ 1:57-80 | ☐ 2:1-8 | ☐ 2:9-20 | ☐ 2:21-39 |
| 19 | ☐ 2:40-52 | ☐ 3:1-20 | ☐ 3:21-38 | ☐ 4:1-13 | ☐ 4:14-30 | ☐ 4:31-44 | ☐ 5:1-26 |
| 20 | ☐ 5:27—6:16 | ☐ 6:17-38 | ☐ 6:39-49 | ☐ 7:1-17 | ☐ 7:18-23 | ☐ 7:24-35 | ☐ 7:36-50 |
| 21 | ☐ 8:1-15 | ☐ 8:16-25 | ☐ 8:26-39 | ☐ 8:40-56 | ☐ 9:1-17 | ☐ 9:18-26 | ☐ 9:27-36 |
| 22 | ☐ 9:37-50 | ☐ 9:51-62 | ☐ 10:1-11 | ☐ 10:12-24 | ☐ 10:25-37 | ☐ 10:38-42 | ☐ 11:1-13 |
| 23 | ☐ 11:14-26 | ☐ 11:27-36 | ☐ 11:37-54 | ☐ 12:1-12 | ☐ 12:13-21 | ☐ 12:22-34 | ☐ 12:35-48 |
| 24 | ☐ 12:49-59 | ☐ 13:1-9 | ☐ 13:10-17 | ☐ 13:18-30 | ☐ 13:31—14:6 | ☐ 14:7-14 | ☐ 14:15-24 |
| 25 | ☐ 14:25-35 | ☐ 15:1-10 | ☐ 15:11-21 | ☐ 15:22-32 | ☐ 16:1-13 | ☐ 16:14-22 | ☐ 16:23-31 |
| 26 | ☐ 17:1-19 | ☐ 17:20-37 | ☐ 18:1-14 | ☐ 18:15-30 | ☐ 18:31-43 | ☐ 19:1-10 | ☐ 19:11-27 |

## Reading Schedule for the Recovery Version of the New Testament with Footnotes

| Wk. | Lord's Day | Monday | Tuesday | Wednesday | Thursday | Friday | Saturday |
|---|---|---|---|---|---|---|---|
| 27 | Luke 19:28-48 | 20:1-19 | 20:20-38 | 20:39—21:4 | 21:5-27 | 21:28-38 | 22:1-20 |
| 28 | 22:21-38 | 22:39-54 | 22:55-71 | 23:1-43 | 23:44-56 | 24:1-12 | 24:13-35 |
| 29 | 24:36-53 | John 1:1-13 | 1:14-18 | 1:19-34 | 1:35-51 | 2:1-11 | 2:12-22 |
| 30 | 2:23—3:13 | 3:14-21 | 3:22-36 | 4:1-14 | 4:15-26 | 4:27-42 | 4:43-54 |
| 31 | 5:1-16 | 5:17-30 | 5:31-47 | 6:1-15 | 6:16-31 | 6:32-51 | 6:52-71 |
| 32 | 7:1-9 | 7:10-24 | 7:25-36 | 7:37-52 | 7:53—8:11 | 8:12-27 | 8:28-44 |
| 33 | 8:45-59 | 9:1-13 | 9:14-34 | 9:35—10:9 | 10:10-30 | 10:31—11:4 | 11:5-22 |
| 34 | 11:23-40 | 11:41-57 | 12:1-11 | 12:12-24 | 12:25-36 | 12:37-50 | 13:1-11 |
| 35 | 13:12-30 | 13:31-38 | 14:1-6 | 14:7-20 | 14:21-31 | 15:1-11 | 15:12-27 |
| 36 | 16:1-15 | 16:16-33 | 17:1-5 | 17:6-13 | 17:14-24 | 17:25—18:11 | 18:12-27 |
| 37 | 18:28-40 | 19:1-16 | 19:17-30 | 19:31-42 | 20:1-13 | 20:14-18 | 20:19-22 |
| 38 | 20:23-31 | 21:1-14 | 21:15-22 | 21:23-25 | Acts 1:1-8 | 1:9-14 | 1:15-26 |
| 39 | 2:1-13 | 2:14-21 | 2:22-36 | 2:37-41 | 2:42-47 | 3:1-18 | 3:19—4:22 |
| 40 | 4:23-37 | 5:1-16 | 5:17-32 | 5:33-42 | 6:1—7:1 | 7:2-29 | 7:30-60 |
| 41 | 8:1-13 | 8:14-25 | 8:26-40 | 9:1-19 | 9:20-43 | 10:1-16 | 10:17-33 |
| 42 | 10:34-48 | 11:1-18 | 11:19-30 | 12:1-25 | 13:1-12 | 13:13-43 | 13:44—14:5 |
| 43 | 14:6-28 | 15:1-12 | 15:13-34 | 15:35—16:5 | 16:6-18 | 16:19-40 | 17:1-18 |
| 44 | 17:19-34 | 18:1-17 | 18:18-28 | 19:1-20 | 19:21-41 | 20:1-12 | 20:13-38 |
| 45 | 21:1-14 | 21:15-26 | 21:27-40 | 22:1-21 | 22:22-29 | 22:30—23:11 | 23:12-15 |
| 46 | 23:16-30 | 23:31—24:21 | 24:22—25:5 | 25:6-27 | 26:1-13 | 26:14-32 | 27:1-26 |
| 47 | 27:27—28:10 | 28:11-22 | 28:23-31 | Rom 1:1-2 | 1:3-7 | 1:8-17 | 1:18-25 |
| 48 | 1:26—2:10 | 2:11-29 | 3:1-20 | 3:21-31 | 4:1-12 | 4:13-25 | 5:1-11 |
| 49 | 5:12-17 | 5:18—6:5 | 6:6-11 | 6:12-23 | 7:1-12 | 7:13-25 | 8:1-2 |
| 50 | 8:3-6 | 8:7-13 | 8:14-25 | 8:26-39 | 9:1-18 | 9:19—10:3 | 10:4-15 |
| 51 | 10:16—11:10 | 11:11-22 | 11:23-36 | 12:1-3 | 12:4-21 | 13:1-14 | 14:1-12 |
| 52 | 14:13-23 | 15:1-13 | 15:14-33 | 16:1-5 | 16:6-24 | 16:25-27 | I Cor 1:1-4 |

# Reading Schedule for the Recovery Version of the New Testament with Footnotes

| Wk. | Lord's Day | Monday | Tuesday | Wednesday | Thursday | Friday | Saturday |
|---|---|---|---|---|---|---|---|
| 53 | ☐ I Cor 1:5-9 | ☐ 1:10-17 | ☐ 1:18-31 | ☐ 2:1-5 | ☐ 2:6-10 | ☐ 2:11-16 | ☐ 3:1-9 |
| 54 | ☐ 3:10-13 | ☐ 3:14-23 | ☐ 4:1-9 | ☐ 4:10-21 | ☐ 5:1-13 | ☐ 6:1-11 | ☐ 6:12-20 |
| 55 | ☐ 7:1-16 | ☐ 7:17-24 | ☐ 7:25-40 | ☐ 8:1-13 | ☐ 9:1-15 | ☐ 9:16-27 | ☐ 10:1-4 |
| 56 | ☐ 10:5-13 | ☐ 10:14-33 | ☐ 11:1-6 | ☐ 11:7-16 | ☐ 11:17-26 | ☐ 11:27-34 | ☐ 12:1-11 |
| 57 | ☐ 12:12-22 | ☐ 12:23-31 | ☐ 13:1-13 | ☐ 14:1-12 | ☐ 14:13-25 | ☐ 14:26-33 | ☐ 14:34-40 |
| 58 | ☐ 15:1-19 | ☐ 15:20-28 | ☐ 15:29-34 | ☐ 15:35-49 | ☐ 15:50-58 | ☐ 16:1-9 | ☐ 16:10-24 |
| 59 | ☐ II Cor 1:1-4 | ☐ 1:5-14 | ☐ 1:15-22 | ☐ 1:23—2:11 | ☐ 2:12-17 | ☐ 3:1-6 | ☐ 3:7-11 |
| 60 | ☐ 3:12-18 | ☐ 4:1-6 | ☐ 4:7-12 | ☐ 4:13-18 | ☐ 5:1-8 | ☐ 5:9-15 | ☐ 5:16-21 |
| 61 | ☐ 6:1-13 | ☐ 6:14—7:4 | ☐ 7:5-16 | ☐ 8:1-15 | ☐ 8:16-24 | ☐ 9:1-15 | ☐ 10:1-6 |
| 62 | ☐ 10:7-18 | ☐ 11:1-15 | ☐ 11:16-33 | ☐ 12:1-10 | ☐ 12:11-21 | ☐ 13:1-10 | ☐ 13:11-14 |
| 63 | ☐ Gal 1:1-5 | ☐ 1:6-14 | ☐ 1:15-24 | ☐ 2:1-13 | ☐ 2:14-21 | ☐ 3:1-4 | ☐ 3:5-14 |
| 64 | ☐ 3:15-22 | ☐ 3:23-29 | ☐ 4:1-7 | ☐ 4:8-20 | ☐ 4:21-31 | ☐ 5:1-12 | ☐ 5:13-21 |
| 65 | ☐ 5:22-26 | ☐ 6:1-10 | ☐ 6:11-15 | ☐ 6:16-18 | ☐ Eph 1:1-3 | ☐ 1:4-6 | ☐ 1:7-10 |
| 66 | ☐ 1:11-14 | ☐ 1:15-18 | ☐ 1:19-23 | ☐ 2:1-5 | ☐ 2:6-10 | ☐ 2:11-14 | ☐ 2:15-18 |
| 67 | ☐ 2:19-22 | ☐ 3:1-7 | ☐ 3:8-13 | ☐ 3:14-18 | ☐ 3:19-21 | ☐ 4:1-4 | ☐ 4:5-10 |
| 68 | ☐ 4:11-16 | ☐ 4:17-24 | ☐ 4:25-32 | ☐ 5:1-10 | ☐ 5:11-21 | ☐ 5:22-26 | ☐ 5:27-33 |
| 69 | ☐ 6:1-9 | ☐ 6:10-14 | ☐ 6:15-18 | ☐ 6:19-24 | ☐ Phil 1:1-7 | ☐ 1:8-18 | ☐ 1:19-26 |
| 70 | ☐ 1:27—2:4 | ☐ 2:5-11 | ☐ 2:12-16 | ☐ 2:17-30 | ☐ 3:1-6 | ☐ 3:7-11 | ☐ 3:12-16 |
| 71 | ☐ 3:17-21 | ☐ 4:1-9 | ☐ 4:10-23 | ☐ Col 1:1-8 | ☐ 1:9-13 | ☐ 1:14-23 | ☐ 1:24-29 |
| 72 | ☐ 2:1-7 | ☐ 2:8-15 | ☐ 2:16-23 | ☐ 3:1-4 | ☐ 3:5-15 | ☐ 3:16-25 | ☐ 4:1-18 |
| 73 | ☐ I Thes 1:1-3 | ☐ 1:4-10 | ☐ 2:1-12 | ☐ 2:13—3:5 | ☐ 3:6-13 | ☐ 4:1-10 | ☐ 4:11—5:11 |
| 74 | ☐ 5:12-28 | ☐ II Thes 1:1-12 | ☐ 2:1-17 | ☐ 3:1-18 | ☐ I Tim 1:1-2 | ☐ 1:3-4 | ☐ 1:5-14 |
| 75 | ☐ 1:15-20 | ☐ 2:1-7 | ☐ 2:8-15 | ☐ 3:1-13 | ☐ 3:14—4:5 | ☐ 4:6-16 | ☐ 5:1-25 |
| 76 | ☐ 6:1-10 | ☐ 6:11-21 | ☐ II Tim 1:1-10 | ☐ 1:11-18 | ☐ 2:1-15 | ☐ 2:16-26 | ☐ 3:1-13 |
| 77 | ☐ 3:14—4:8 | ☐ 4:9-22 | ☐ Titus 1:1-4 | ☐ 1:5-16 | ☐ 2:1-15 | ☐ 3:1-8 | ☐ 3:9-15 |
| 78 | ☐ Philem 1:1-11 | ☐ 1:12-25 | ☐ Heb 1:1-2 | ☐ 1:3-5 | ☐ 1:6-14 | ☐ 2:1-9 | ☐ 2:10-18 |

# Reading Schedule for the Recovery Version of the New Testament with Footnotes

| Wk. | Lord's Day | Monday | Tuesday | Wednesday | Thursday | Friday | Saturday |
|---|---|---|---|---|---|---|---|
| 79 | Heb 3:1-6 | 3:7-19 | 4:1-9 | 4:10-13 | 4:14-16 | 5:1-10 | 5:11—6:3 |
| 80 | 6:4-8 | 6:9-20 | 7:1-10 | 7:11-28 | 8:1-6 | 8:7-13 | 9:1-4 |
| 81 | 9:5-14 | 9:15-28 | 10:1-18 | 10:19-28 | 10:29-39 | 11:1-6 | 11:7-19 |
| 82 | 11:20-31 | 11:32-40 | 12:1-2 | 12:3-13 | 12:14-17 | 12:18-26 | 12:27-29 |
| 83 | 13:1-7 | 13:8-12 | 13:13-15 | 13:16-25 | James 1:1-8 | 1:9-18 | 1:19-27 |
| 84 | 2:1-13 | 2:14-26 | 3:1-18 | 4:1-10 | 4:11-17 | 5:1-12 | 5:13-20 |
| 85 | I Pet 1:1-2 | 1:3-4 | 1:5 | 1:6-9 | 1:10-12 | 1:13-17 | 1:18-25 |
| 86 | 2:1-3 | 2:4-8 | 2:9-17 | 2:18-25 | 3:1-13 | 3:14-22 | 4:1-6 |
| 87 | 4:7-16 | 4:17-19 | 5:1-4 | 5:5-9 | 5:10-14 | II Pet 1:1-2 | 1:3-4 |
| 88 | 1:5-8 | 1:9-11 | 1:12-18 | 1:19-21 | 2:1-3 | 2:4-11 | 2:12-22 |
| 89 | 3:1-6 | 3:7-9 | 3:10-12 | 3:13-15 | 3:16 | 3:17-18 | I John 1:1-2 |
| 90 | 1:3-4 | 1:5 | 1:6 | 1:7 | 1:8-10 | 2:1-2 | 2:3-11 |
| 91 | 2:12-14 | 2:15-19 | 2:20-23 | 2:24-27 | 2:28-29 | 3:1-5 | 3:6-10 |
| 92 | 3:11-18 | 3:19-24 | 4:1-6 | 4:7-11 | 4:12-15 | 4:16—5:3 | 5:4-13 |
| 93 | 5:14-17 | 5:18-21 | II John 1:1-3 | 1:4-9 | 1:10-13 | III John 1:1-6 | 1:7-14 |
| 94 | Jude 1:1-4 | 1:5-10 | 1:11-19 | 1:20-25 | Rev 1:1-3 | 1:4-6 | 1:7-11 |
| 95 | 1:12-13 | 1:14-16 | 1:17-20 | 2:1-6 | 2:7 | 2:8-9 | 2:10-11 |
| 96 | 2:12-14 | 2:15-17 | 2:18-23 | 2:24-29 | 3:1-3 | 3:4-6 | 3:7-9 |
| 97 | 3:10-13 | 3:14-18 | 3:19-22 | 4:1-5 | 4:6-7 | 4:8-11 | 5:1-6 |
| 98 | 5:7-14 | 6:1-8 | 6:9-17 | 7:1-8 | 7:9-17 | 8:1-6 | 8:7-12 |
| 99 | 8:13—9:11 | 9:12-21 | 10:1-4 | 10:5-11 | 11:1-4 | 11:5-14 | 11:15-19 |
| 100 | 12:1-4 | 12:5-9 | 12:10-18 | 13:1-10 | 13:11-18 | 14:1-5 | 14:6-12 |
| 101 | 14:13-20 | 15:1-8 | 16:1-12 | 16:13-21 | 17:1-6 | 17:7-18 | 18:1-8 |
| 102 | 18:9—19:4 | 19:5-10 | 19:11-16 | 19:17-21 | 20:1-6 | 20:7-10 | 20:11-15 |
| 103 | 21:1 | 21:2 | 21:3-8 | 21:9-13 | 21:14-18 | 21:19-21 | 21:22-27 |
| 104 | 22:1 | 22:2 | 22:3-11 | 22:12-15 | 22:16-17 | 22:18-21 | |

## Week 1 — Day 1

**Today's verses**

1 Tim. 1:3-4  Even as I exhorted you...to remain in Ephesus in order that you might charge certain ones not to teach different things,...which produce questionings rather than God's economy, which is in faith.

Eph. 3:9-11  And to enlighten all *that they may see* what the economy of the mystery is, which throughout the ages has been hidden in God, who created all things, in order that now to the rulers and the authorities in the heavenlies the multifarious wisdom of God might be made known through the church, according to the eternal purpose which He made in Christ Jesus our Lord.

_____
Date

## Week 1 — Day 2

**Today's verses**

John 1:14  And the Word became flesh and tabernacled among us (and we beheld His glory, glory as of the only Begotten from the Father), full of grace and reality.

12:24  ...Unless the grain of wheat falls into the ground and dies, it abides alone; but if it dies, it bears much fruit.

3:3  ...Unless one is born anew, he cannot see the kingdom of God.

29  He who has the bride is the bridegroom...

_____
Date

## Week 1 — Day 3

**Today's verses**

2 Pet. 1:4  Through which He has granted to us precious and exceedingly great promises that through these you might become partakers of the divine nature...

1 John 3:1-2  Behold what manner of love the Father has given to us, that we should be called children of God; and we are....And it has not yet been manifested what we will be. We know that if He is manifested, we will be like Him because we will see Him even as He is.

Rev. 21:10  And he...showed me the holy city, Jerusalem, coming down out of heaven from God.

_____
Date

## Week 1 — Day 4

**Today's verses**

Eph. 4:14-15  That we may be no longer little children tossed by waves and carried about by every wind of teaching in the sleight of men, in craftiness with a view to a system of error, but holding to truth in love, we may grow up into Him in all things, who is the Head, Christ.

Gal. 6:15  For neither is circumcision anything nor uncircumcision, but a new creation *is what matters.*

2 Cor. 5:17  So then if anyone is in Christ, *he is* a new creation. The old things have passed away; behold, they have become new.

_____
Date

## Week 1 — Day 5

**Today's verses**

1 Tim. 1:3-4  Even as I exhorted you...that you might charge certain ones not to teach different things,...rather than God's economy, which is in faith.

Rom. 10:17  So faith *comes* out of hearing, and hearing through the word of Christ.

Eph. 3:9  And to enlighten all *that they may see* what the economy of the mystery is...

Heb. 12:2  Looking away unto Jesus, the Author and Perfecter of our faith, who for the joy set before Him endured the cross, despising the shame, and has sat down on the right hand of the throne of God.

_____
Date

## Week 1 — Day 6

**Today's verses**

1 Tim. 1:3  Even as I exhorted you, when I was going into Macedonia, to remain in Ephesus in order that you might charge certain ones not to teach different things.

6:3  If anyone teaches different things and does not consent to healthy words, those of our Lord Jesus Christ, and the teaching which is according to godliness.

Titus 1:9  Holding to the faithful word, which is according to the teaching *of the apostles,* that he may be able both to exhort by the healthy teaching and to convict those who oppose.

_____
Date

## Week 2 — Day 4 — Today's verses

Eph. In whom all the building, being fitted to-
2:21-22 gether, is growing into a holy temple in
the Lord; in whom you also are being
built together into a dwelling place of
God in spirit.

4:15 But holding to truth in love, we may grow
up into Him in all things, who is the Head,
Christ.

1 Pet. As newborn babes, long for the guileless
2:2 milk of the word in order that by it you
may grow unto salvation.

5 You yourselves also, as living stones, are
being built up as a spiritual house…

_____
Date

## Week 2 — Day 5 — Today's verses

John In My Father's house are many abodes; if *it*
14:2 *were not so*, I would have told you; for I go to
prepare a place for you.

23 …If anyone loves Me, he will keep My word,
and My Father will love him, and We will
come to him and make an abode with him.

Eph. …You are fellow citizens with the saints and
2:19-20 members of the household of God, being
built upon the foundation of the apostles and
prophets, Christ Jesus Himself being the cornerstone.

3:16-17 That He would grant you…to be strengthened with power through His Spirit into the
inner man, that Christ may make His home
in your hearts through faith…

_____
Date

## Week 2 — Day 6 — Today's verses

John In My Father's house are many abodes; if
14:2 *it were not so*, I would have told you; for I
go to prepare a place for you.

1 Tim. But if I delay, I *write* that you may know
3:15 how one ought to conduct himself in the
house of God, which is the church of the
living God, the pillar and base of the
truth.

2 Tim. But in a great house there are not only
2:20 gold and silver vessels but also wooden
and earthen; and some are unto honor,
and some are unto dishonor.

_____
Date

## Week 2 — Day 1 — Today's verses

Acts Take heed to yourselves and to all the
20:28 flock, among whom the Holy Spirit has
placed you as overseers to shepherd the
church of God, which He obtained
through His own blood.

2 Cor. But I, I will most gladly spend and be ut-
12:15 terly spent on behalf of your souls. If I love
you more abundantly, am I loved less?

11:28 …There is this: the crowd of cares pressing upon me daily, the anxious concern
for all the churches.

_____
Date

## Week 2 — Day 2 — Today's verses

1 Tim. …The house of God, which is the church
3:15-16 of the living God….And confessedly,
great is the mystery of godliness: He who
was manifested in the flesh,…

Eph. And He subjected all things under His
1:22-23 feet and gave Him *to be* Head over all
things to the church, which is His Body,
the fullness of the One who fills all in all.

2:19 So then you are no longer strangers and
sojourners, but you are fellow citizens
with the saints and members of the household of God.

_____
Date

## Week 2 — Day 3 — Today's verses

John Even as You have given Him authority
17:2-3 over all flesh to give eternal life to all
whom You have given Him. And this is
eternal life, that they may know You, the
only true God, and Him whom You have
sent, Jesus Christ.

11 …Holy Father, keep them in Your name,
which You have given to Me, that they
may be one even as We are.

1 Pet. Blessed be the God and Father of our Lord
1:3 Jesus Christ, who according to His great
mercy has regenerated us unto a living
hope through the resurrection of Jesus
Christ from the dead.

_____
Date

## Week 3 — Day 4     Today's verses

1 Tim.  ...The house of God, which is the church
3:15  of the living God, the pillar and base of the truth.

Matt.  And Simon Peter answered and said, You
16:16  are the Christ, the Son of the living God.
18  And I also say to you that you are Peter, and upon this rock I will build My church, and the gates of Hades shall not prevail against it.

Eph.  This mystery is great, but I speak with re-
5:32  gard to Christ and the church.

*Date*

---

## Week 3 — Day 5     Today's verses

2 Tim.  Be diligent to present yourself approved
2:15  to God, an unashamed workman, cutting straight the word of the truth.
25  In meekness correcting those who oppose, if perhaps God may give them repentance unto the full knowledge of the truth.

Titus  Paul, a slave of God and an apostle of Je-
1:1  sus Christ according to the faith of God's chosen ones and the full knowledge of the truth, which is according to godliness.

*Date*

---

## Week 3 — Day 6     Today's verses

1 Cor.  But in the church I would rather speak five
14:19-20  words with my mind, that I might instruct others also, than ten thousand words in a tongue. Brothers, do not be children in *your* understanding, but in malice be babes and in your understanding be full-grown.

1 Tim.  Who desires all men to be saved and to
2:4  come to the full knowledge of the truth.
3:15  ...*I write* that you may know how one ought to conduct himself in the house of God, which is the church of the living God, the pillar and base of the truth.

*Date*

---

## Week 3 — Day 1     Today's verses

1 Tim.  ...*I write* that you may know how one ought
3:15  to conduct himself in the house of God, which is the church of the living God, the pillar and base of the truth.

2 Tim.  However the firm foundation of God stands,
2:19  having this seal, The Lord knows those who are His, and, Let everyone who names the name of the Lord depart from unrighteousness.

Rev.  And the living One; and I became dead, and
1:18  behold, I am living forever and ever; and I have the keys of death and of Hades.

Matt.  And I also say to you that you are Peter, and
16:18  upon this rock I will build My church, and the gates of Hades shall not prevail against it.

*Date*

---

## Week 3 — Day 2     Today's verses

John  Jesus said to him, I am the way and the re-
14:6  ality and the life; no one comes to the Father except through Me.
1:4  In Him was life, and the life was the light of men.
8:32  And you shall know the truth, and the truth shall set you free.
17:17  Sanctify them in the truth; Your word is truth.

*Date*

---

## Week 3 — Day 3     Today's verses

John  Again therefore Jesus spoke to them, say-
8:12  ing, I am the light of the world; he who follows Me shall by no means walk in darkness, but shall have the light of life.
32  And you shall know the truth, and the truth shall set you free.
36  If therefore the Son sets you free, you shall be free indeed.

*Date*

**Week 4 — Day 6**                    Today's verses

Rev. And he carried me away in spirit onto a
21:10-11 great and high mountain and showed me
the holy city, Jerusalem, coming down
out of heaven from God, having the glory
of God. Her light was like a most precious
stone, like a jasper stone, as clear as crystal.

18  And the building work of its wall was jasper; and the city was pure gold, like clear
glass.

23  And the city has no need of the sun or of
the moon that they should shine in it, for
the glory of God illumined it, and its lamp
is the Lamb.

_____
Date

---

**Week 4 — Day 5**                    Today's verses

John I am the vine; you are the branches. He
15:5 who abides in Me and I in him, he bears
much fruit; for apart from Me you can do
nothing.

Eph. And put on the new man, which was cre-
4:24 ated according to God in righteousness
and holiness of the reality.

1 Cor. But he who is joined to the Lord is one
6:17 spirit.

_____
Date

---

**Week 4 — Day 4**                    Today's verses

1 Tim. ...In the house of God, which is the
3:15-16 church of the living God, the pillar and
base of the truth. And confessedly, great is
the mystery of godliness: He who was
manifested in the flesh, justified in the
Spirit, seen by angels, preached among
the nations, believed on in the world,
taken up in glory.

Gal. I am crucified with Christ; and *it is* no lon-
2:20 ger I *who* live, but *it is* Christ *who* lives in
me; and the *life* which I now live in the
flesh I live in faith, the *faith* of the Son of
God, who loved me and gave Himself up
for me.

_____
Date

---

**Week 4 — Day 3**                    Today's verses

1 Tim. But if I delay, *I write* that you may know
3:15-16 how one ought to conduct himself in the
house of God, which is the church of the
living God, the pillar and base of the
truth. And confessedly, great is the mystery of godliness: He who was manifested
in the flesh, justified in the Spirit, seen by
angels, preached among the nations, believed on in the world, taken up in glory.

1 Cor. But if all prophesy and some unbeliever
14:24-25 or unlearned person enters, he is convicted by all, he is examined by all; the secrets of his heart become manifest; and so
falling on *his* face, he will worship God,
declaring that indeed God is among you.

_____
Date

---

**Week 4 — Day 2**                    Today's verses

John In the beginning was the Word, and the
1:1 Word was with God, and the Word was
God.

14  And the Word became flesh and tabernacled among us (and we beheld His
glory, glory as of the only Begotten from
the Father), full of grace and reality.

14:10 Do you not believe that I am in the Father
and the Father is in Me?...

_____
Date

---

**Week 4 — Day 1**                    Today's verses

Eph. Predestinating us unto sonship through
1:5 Jesus Christ to Himself, according to the
good pleasure of His will.

9  Making known to us the mystery of His
will according to His good pleasure,
which He purposed in Himself.

Col. For in Him dwells all the fullness of the
2:9 Godhead bodily.

_____
Date

## Week 5 — Day 6 — Today's verses

Heb. 4:12 For the word of God is living and operative and sharper than any two-edged sword, and piercing even to the dividing of soul and spirit,...and able to discern the thoughts and intentions of the heart.

Matt. 16:25 For whoever wants to save his soul-life shall lose it; but whoever loses his soul-life for My sake shall find it.

2 Tim. 2:22 But flee youthful lusts, and pursue righteousness, faith, love, peace with those who call on the Lord out of a pure heart.

*Date* _____

## Week 5 — Day 5 — Today's verses

Mal. 2:16 ...Take heed then to your spirit, and do not be treacherous.

Rom. 8:6 For the mind set on the flesh is death, but the mind set on the spirit is life and peace.

2 Cor. 2:13 I had no rest in my spirit, for I did not find Titus my brother....

*Date* _____

## Week 5 — Day 4 — Today's verses

1 Tim. 2:1-3 I exhort therefore, first of all, that petitions, prayers, intercessions, thanksgivings be made on behalf of all men; on behalf of kings and all who are in high position, that we may lead a quiet and tranquil life in all godliness and gravity. This is good and acceptable in the sight of our Savior God.

8 I desire therefore that men pray in every place, lifting up holy hands, without wrath and reasoning.

*Date* _____

## Week 5 — Day 3 — Today's verses

2 Tim. 1:6-7 For which cause I remind you to fan into flame the gift of God, which is in you through the laying on of my hands. For God has not given us a spirit of cowardice, but of power and of love and of sobermindedness.

Rom. 12:11 Do not be slothful in zeal, *but* be burning in spirit, serving the Lord.

*Date* _____

## Week 5 — Day 2 — Today's verses

1 Tim. 4:7-8 But the profane and old-womanish myths refuse, and exercise yourself unto godliness. For bodily exercise is profitable for a little, but godliness is profitable for all things, having promise of the present life and of that which is to come.

2 Tim. 1:6-7 For which cause I remind you to fan into flame the gift of God, which is in you through the laying on of my hands. For God has not given us a spirit of cowardice, but of power and of love and of sobermindedness.

*Date* _____

## Week 5 — Day 1 — Today's verses

Zech. 12:1 *Thus* declares Jehovah, who stretches forth the heavens and lays the foundations of the earth and forms the spirit of man within him.

Gen. 2:7 Jehovah God formed man from the dust of the ground and breathed into his nostrils the breath of life, and man became a living soul.

John 4:24 God is Spirit, and those who worship Him must worship in spirit and truthfulness.

1 Cor. 6:17 But he who is joined to the Lord is one spirit.

*Date* _____

**Week 6 — Day 4**                              Today's verses

1 Cor. Now I beseech you, brothers, through the
1:10 name of our Lord Jesus Christ, that you all
speak the same thing and *that* there be no
divisions among you, but *that* you be attuned in the same mind and in the same
opinion.

15:45 ...The last Adam *became* a life-giving
Spirit.

Eph. This mystery is great, but I speak with re-
5:32 gard to Christ and the church.

_____
*Date*

---

**Week 6 — Day 5**                              Today's verses

2 Cor. For I am jealous over you with a jealousy
11:2-3 of God; for I betrothed you to one husband to present *you* as a pure virgin to
Christ. But I fear lest somehow, as the serpent deceived Eve by his craftiness, your
thoughts would be corrupted from the
simplicity and the purity toward Christ.

Col. I now rejoice in my sufferings on your be-
1:24 half and fill up on my part that which is
lacking of the afflictions of Christ in my
flesh for His Body, which is the church.

_____
*Date*

---

**Week 6 — Day 6**                              Today's verses

2 Tim. For which cause also I suffer these things;
1:12-14 but I am not ashamed, for I know whom I
have believed, and I am persuaded that
He is able to guard my deposit unto that
day. Hold a pattern of the healthy words
that you have heard from me, in the faith
and love which are in Christ Jesus. Guard
the good deposit through the Holy Spirit
who dwells in us.

_____
*Date*

---

**Week 6 — Day 1**                              Today's verses

Col. Of which I became a minister according
1:25-26 to the stewardship of God, which was
given to me for you, to complete the word
of God, the mystery which has been hidden from the ages and from the genera-
tions but now has been manifested to His
saints.

28-29 Whom we announce, admonishing every
man and teaching every man in all wisdom that we may present every man
full-grown in Christ; for which also I labor, struggling according to His operation
which operates in me in power.

_____
*Date*

---

**Week 6 — Day 2**                              Today's verses

2 Tim. This you know, that all who are in Asia
1:15 turned away from me, of whom are
Phygelus and Hermogenes.

Rev. But I have *one thing* against you, that you
2:4 have left your first love.

3:16 So, because you are lukewarm and neither hot nor cold, I am about to spew you
out of My mouth.

_____
*Date*

---

**Week 6 — Day 3**                              Today's verses

1 Tim. If anyone teaches different things and
6:3-4 does not consent to healthy words, those
of our Lord Jesus Christ, and the teaching
which is according to godliness, he is
blinded with pride, understanding nothing, but is diseased with questionings and
contentions of words, out of which come
envy, strife, slanders, evil suspicions.

Rev. I know your works; behold, I have put be-
3:8 fore you an opened door which no one
can shut, because you have a little power
and have kept My word and have not denied My name.

_____
*Date*